THE PILGRIM CHURCH

THE
PILGRIM CHURCH

George H. Tavard

HERDER AND HERDER

_103980_

1967
HERDER AND HERDER NEW YORK
232 Madison Avenue, New York, 10016

Nihil obstat: Thomas J. Beary, Censor Librorum
Imprimatur: ✠Robert F. Joyce, Bishop of Burington
May 1, 1967

Library of Congress Catalogue Card Number: 67–25886
© 1967 by Herder and Herder, Inc.
Manufactured in the United States of America

Contents

To
Judy Contrucci
Kathy Sweeney
Pat Gorman
Cindy Keller

Foreword

THE BOOKS written about the Second Council of the Vatican are
bound to belong to several successive "genres." So far, four main
kinds seem to have been published. There have been volumes
expressing desires and projects relevant to the renovation of
Church life to be effected by the Council, the type of which may
be taken to be Hans Küng's *The Council, Reform and Reunion.*
A second sort of publication falls in the long traditonal, yet today
hardly practiced, "genre" of the objective chronicle of events, of
which an outstanding example will be found in the volumes of
Antoine Wenger: *Vatican II,* which record and explain the facts
of the Council session by session. A third kind of book about the
Vatican Council embodies the partisan approach to, and interpretation of, history, the best known instance of which is Xavier
Rynne's *Letters from Vatican City.* A fourth kind, and the last
which I have observed so far, is the published diary of an eye-
witness: we may cite Douglas Horton's *Vatican Diary* as an il-
luminating example of this sort of document.

The publication of the decrees and constitutions of the Council
calls for another and more lasting look at its achievements, in
order to study the work of the Vatican Fathers in its theological
depth. The odd turmoil of the beginning post-conciliar area, in
which the feet-draggers become reactionary and the impatients

9

join the lunatic fringe, points to the need for serenity in assessing the *kairos* of Vatican II. The present essay has been written as an initiation into this dimension of the Council. It investigates some of the major themes of the Constitution on the Church, promulgated at the end of the third session of the Council (November 1964).

One should not look for a complete study of the Vatican Council's ecclesiology in these pages. It would still be premature to attempt a definitive work on this major topic, for only developments yet to come will enable us to perceive the full dimension of the Vatican Council's documents. Evidently, the insights of those who participated in the debates in St Peter's Basilica and in the hard work of the relevant commissions and sub-commissions will be needed for adequate historical studies on the Second Vatican Council. Nonetheless, the content and meaning of the texts that were officially endorsed are not to be gathered merely from the points of view that entered into their composition. We also need to hear their echo as it sounds back and forth in the Church's self-awareness, as the decisions of the Council begin to bear fruit. I have therefore tried to help readers to attune their ears to these echoes, hoping that their reading of the texts of the Council may be for them a rich spiritual experience.

* * *

Part of the first chapter was read at a symposium at the University of California in Santa Barbara in the spring of 1966. Chapters two to five were prepared as the Swander Lectures at Lancaster Theological Seminary in March 1967. The first half of Chapter Six was read before the clergy of the diocese of Youngstown, Ohio, in the spring of 1966. Chapter Seven is reproduced from *Worship* (January 1965).

Center for Advanced Studies
Wesleyan University, Middletown, Conn.   George H. Tavard

THE PILGRIM CHURCH

I.

The Theological Setting of Vatican II

IN 1954, a book by a Belgian theologian of note, Roger Aubert, bore the title, *Catholic Theology in the Middle of the Twentieth Century*.[1] On account of its timing and topic, this provides a significant panorama of Catholic theology shortly before the Vatican Council. In its 101 pages I have found references to 114 French-language books and authors, to 20 German, five Dutch or Flemish and one Italian book. No reference to English or American authors.

From this we may gather that it is possible to give a reasonably accurate picture of the theological situation before John XXIII by

1. *La Théologie Catholique au milieu du XXe Siècle*, Paris, 1954. Compare with Jean Daniélou: "Les orientations présentes de la pensée religieuse" (*Etudes*, 1946, pp. 5–21); Yves Congar: "Tendances actuelles de la pensée religieuse" (*Cahiers du Monde Nouveau*, 1948, pp. 33–50); James M. Connolly: *The Voices of France. A Survey of Contemporary Theology in France*, New York, 1961; Elmer O'Brien (ed.): *Theology in Transition, A Bibliographical Evaluation of the "Decisive Decade," 1954–1964*, New York, 1965; James Schall and Donald Wolf: *Current Trends in Theology*, 1966.

referring mainly to writers in the French and German languages. Assuredly, one could have made other quotations and referred to other works. The several language groups of the Catholic world would then have been featured in different proportions. I myself would have included more German and Austrian titles. On the whole, however, the emphasis adopted by Aubert was correct and the corresponding allusions to national or linguistic contributions to theology were true to facts. Catholic theological leadership before 1962 was reduced to France and Germany and the neighboring smaller countries. The situation is largely unchanged today, although I would think that German writing, which came second before the Council, has now gained the first place.

Other language groups were affected by theological problems mainly through German- or French-speaking theologians. For instance, Spain after the Civil War made a remarkable theological effort, to which the publications of *Biblioteca de Auctores Cristianos* bear witness. Yet this effort, so far, has produced editions and translations of patristic and medieval texts, editions of theological classics, translations from the French and German, a number of text-books, but relatively little in the field of original research. In the English-speaking world, theological research came first in England, with the high scholarship of the *Bellarmine Series*. The United States lagged behind, in spite of the valuable but very specialized productions of the *Franciscan Institute* and the distinguished contributions of *Theological Studies*.

This disproportion of theological activity in the various language groups of the Catholic world naturally corresponded to a lack of balance in the intellectual, and I would add, spiritual level of Catholic life. The various crises that shook Catholicism in France

16

and elsewhere during and after the Second World War had their origins in this imbalance rather than in anything intrinsic to the Church in France.

Let me briefly recall these crises, in order to eliminate the painful part of my task first and to proceed to deeper considerations. In 1941 the Holy Office placed on the Index a book by M. D. Chenu: *Une Ecole de Théologie: le Saulchoir,* and took the author away from his function as Regent of Studies at Le Saulchoir. The basic objection seems to have been that the theological method described and advocated in this book was not sufficiently close to the conservative understanding of Thomism held by some prominent professors in Roman universities.

This was but a foretaste of worse things to come. In 1950 the encyclical *Humani Generis* was published, and restrictive measures were adopted by the Holy Office against several theologians of the Society of Jesus, the main one being Henri de Lubac, who was removed from his teaching in the Jesuit scholasticate and the Catholic Faculties of Lyons. This seems to have been the direct outcome of a violent polemic launched in 1946–47 by Reginald Garrigou-Lagrange against what he called "the new theology," an expression coined by himself and rejected by those whom he thus labeled.

In 1952 a new crisis that was both theological and political erupted when the Assembly of French Cardinals and Archbishops addressed serious warnings to the movement called *Jeunesse de l'Eglise,* and Father Montuclard's small volume, *Les Evènements et la Foi,* was condemned by the Holy Office on account of the rather obvious and all too crude Marxist tendency of the book. This famous question of the "progressist movement" was to have later sequels affecting the priest-workers, many of whom, however, were unconnected with *Jeunesse de l'Eglise* and did not share Montuclard's contention that the establishment of some sort of Communist society was an indispensable prerequisite to the evangelization of modern man. The priest-worker experiment, started by Cardinal Emmanuel Suhard in 1941, was suppressed by Pope Pius XII in 1953, when the Pope imposed conditions that made the priests' work practically impossible. In 1959 Pope John cleared the situation by officially pronouncing the ending of the experiment.[2] It is known today that Pope Paul VI has permitted its resumption.[3]

While all this was taking place at the level of the Church's attempt to renovate her methods of evangelization, restrictive measures similar to those formerly taken against Henri de Lubac hit one of the dominant figures of French theology, the Dominican Yves Congar, who was removed from teaching, prohibited from publishing and who spent some time in exile in various houses of his Order in Jerusalem, Rome and Cambridge. The three French provincials of the Order of Preachers were hastily removed from their functions.

These historical events were of primary importance in the preparation of the Council, in that they showed the embattled atmosphere of the last decade of the pontificate of Pius XII. Pope John injected a good dose of serenity into the theological world when he adopted a lackadaisical attitude which contrasted so

2. Letter from Cardinal Giuseppe Pizzardo to Cardinal Maurice Feltin, July 3, 1959 (text in *Documentation Catholique,* 1959, n. 1313, cols. 1221–1226); letters from John XXIII to Cardinal Paul Richaud (October 29, 1959) and to Archbishop Guerry (same date) (text in *l. c.,* 1960, n. 1319, cols. 11–12).

3. Statement made by the National Conference of the French Bishops, October 23, 1965 (text in *l.c.,* 1965, n. 1459, col. 1989).

much with the sternness of his predecessor. But the old battles were likely to be fought all over again in the aula of St. Peter and in the lobbies of the Vatican Council, if any of the clashing tendencies tried to gain a sizable advantage over its opponent.

These crises were related to the theological movement which started in France during World War II and flourished after the War. This was so far from being a purely academic renewal that Yves Congar has written: "He who did not experience the years 1946–47 of French Catholicism has missed one of the most beautiful moments of the life of the Church."[4] This "moment" and the thought which gave it life were a compound of several factors, which Roger Aubert's volume brings under four broad headings: —Biblical renewal; —liturgical and patristic renewal; —openness to the modern world; —facing existentialism and ecumenism. In each of these fields he analyzes the tendencies of the most important writers. My effort here will be less analytical. It is important to know *what* is done and written; it is valuable too to realize *how* and *why* it is done. I will therefore attempt a genetic approach, showing how, from a basic point, common to much contemporary theology, a number of paths have converged toward the crossroads of the Vatican Council.

* * *

One of the significant controversies of our century, which was largely an intra-Thomist question, centered on a historical point: Did St. Thomas identify *doctrina sacra* with Holy Scripture or with theological speculation? Is the Thomistic *habitus,* that is,

4. *Chrétiens en Dialogue. Contributions à l'oecuménisme,* Paris, 1964, p. *xliii.*

the theory and practice, of theological reflection formally distinct from that of faith? Among others, M. D. Chenu and M.-R. Gagnebet affirmed the distinction. Jean-Francois Bonnefoy denied it, maintaining that the distinction, which is necessary to the transcendence of faith above human reflection, had been introduced into theology by St. Bonaventure and neglected by St. Thomas. Chenu, who published *La Théologie comme Science au XIIIe siècle* in 1943, *Introduction à l'Etude de saint Thomas d'Aquin* in 1950, and *La Théologie est-elle une science?* in 1957, has not, as far as I can see, done away with Bonnefoy's objections. Dom Paul de Vooght has shown that, whatever Aquinas may have said, the fourteenth and fifteenth centuries still equated Scripture with theology.[5]

This controversy was by no means a mere quarrel about words. It does ask if the term *scientia* can be properly applied to theology. It also delves into a point of historical information concerning what exactly St. Thomas thought of the nature of theology. Yet there is more to it than meets the eye: the very nature and method of theological work are at stake.

Is theology today the remnant or the continuation of a speculative system based on the data of revelation, analogous to what scholastic philosophy tries to be in relation to the data of natural experience? Should we answer this question affirmatively we must support and develop the system that satisfies us best— Thomism, Scotism or any other—and beware of everything that

5. M. D. Chenu: *La Théologie comme Science au XIIIe Siècle*, 3rd ed., Paris, 1957; M. R. Gagnebet: "La nature de la théologie spéculative" (*Revue Thomiste*, vol. 34, pp. 1–39, 213–255, 645–674); Jean François Bonnefoy: *La Nature de la Théologie selon saint Thomas d'Aquin*, 1929; Paul de Vooght: *Les Sources de la Doctrine Chrétienne*, 1954; M. D. Chenu: *Is Theology a Science?*, New York, 1959; *La Foi dans l'Intelligence*, 1964.

does not easily fall within our categories. Or is theology a reflection, not only on the past datum of the Gospel as embodied in Scripture and the Church's tradition, but also on the spiritual experience of Christians today, as it was formerly a reflection on Christian experience then?

This, I believe, has been the fundamental theological problem of our century. It has been discussed mainly in France, from the time of Modernism to our own. Yet Germany raised it, though in rather different terms, with its pre-war debate on "kerygmatic" theology.[6]

From this vantage point, a number of perspectives were opened, of which I will indicate a few.

The medieval problem of the place of Holy Scripture in theology reappeared in a modern form when the meaning of the decree of the Council of Trent on Scripture and the Traditions was re-examined by Edmond Ortigues in 1949. The longer and more documented studies of Joseph Geiselmann followed ten years later. Theologians as different as Guy de Broglie and Yves Congar contributed to the growing literature of the question of tradition. When Joseph Hugh Crehan writes that "the evidence is against" their interpretation of Trent, I am sorry to see him show that he is badly misinformed.[7] But the question is not merely one of historical interest. It concerns the place to be given Scripture in our theology. The reinterpretation of the Council of Trent has released a pent-up desire to approach the Scriptures as speaking Word rather than as source-book of information. The

6. J. A. Jungmann: *The Good News Yesterday and Today,* 1962 (German publication, 1936).

7. "Theological Trends," in Elmer O'Brien, *l. c.,* p. 12. Bibliography in Gabriel Moran: *Scripture and Tradition. A Survey of the Controversy,* 1963.

various "biblical theologies" in the making, and the increasing interest in a theology of the spoken and written Word, testify that historical investigations of Scripture and Tradition have had their effect in the renovation of our theology.[8]

This return to the Bible goes hand in hand with a general return to the patristic sources of the Catholic tradition. Illustrated in literature by Lanza del Vasto[9] and others, the wish to make our pilgrimage up-stream to the sources we come from has been implemented in the various renewals of patristic studies, of liturgics, of the theology of the mysteries, of mystical theology. The French series of patristic and medieval monastic texts, *Sources Chrétiennes,* stands as an eloquent monument to this search. The life work of Daniélou and de Lubac has shown the vitality of this line of thinking.

It goes without saying that such a "return to the sources" brings into question the validity of scholasticism and especially Thomism as a "perennial" theology.[10] This point caused enough

8. Louis Bouyer: *Du Protestantisme à l'Eglise,* Paris, 1954 (ET: *The Spirit and Forms of Protestantism,* Westminster, 1956), with an appendix by Guy de Broglie on "the primacy of the argument from Scripture in theology." Among more recent productions: Otto Semmelroth: *The Preaching Word,* New York, 1964; Hans Urs von Balthasar: *Word and Revelation,* New York, 1964; E. Schillebeeckx: *Openbaring en Theologie,* 1965; Luis Alonso Schökel: *The Inspired Word,* New York, 1965.

9. *Le Pélerinage aux Sources,* Paris, 1943.

10. The controversy was sparked by Henri Bouillard's conclusion to his volume: *Conversion et Grâce chez saint Thomas d'Aquin,* Paris, 1944. See Henri Bouillard: "Notes sur le développement de la théologie" (*L'Année Théologique,* 1946, pp. 254–262); an editorial in *Recherches de Science Religieuse:* "La théologie et ses sources. Réponse à la 'Revue Thomiste'," vol. 33, 1946, pp. 385–401); Henri de Lubac: "Le problème du développement du dogme" (*Recherches de Science Religieuse,* vol. 35, 1948, pp. 130–160), with full bibliography. The opposite point of view is ably presented by M. L. Guérard des Lauriers: "La théologie historique et le développement de la théologie" (*L'Année Théologique,* 1946, pp. 15–55).

anxiety among Roman circles to occasion the inclusion of a defense of *philosophia perennis* in the encyclical *Humani Generis,* 1950 (D.S., 3894). But several parts of this encyclical were already out of date when they were written. In particular, its description of theological work did not at all correspond to the practice of theology and the self-reflection of the theological mind upon itself: "Their task is to indicate in what way the teaching of the living magisterium is found, explicitly or implicitly, in the Sacred Scriptures and the divine tradition" (D.S., 3886). Theology today, like theology in the 13th century itself, is much more than a search for the traditional and biblical sources of the teachings of the magisterium.[11] The theological relevance of Thomism's philosophical assumptions is an old question, already raised when the bishop of Paris, Etienne Tempier, condemned several propositions culled from the works of St. Thomas. Lately, however, we have been concerned with a more basic principle than Tempier was. What Tempier feared was the new which appeared in Thomism. We are now concerned with the old in it: the historical development of theology would seem to invalidate some of the philosophical categories formerly in use in theological elaboration. The matter came to a head with *Humani Generis,* which had at least the good effect of slowing the polemics down and inducing theologians to look at the question with further deliberation.

Just as modern times have brought Thomism into question, it has ushered the sciences within the realm of theology. The same logic has been at work in both instances. Although the works of Pierre Teilhard de Chardin have been printed in book form only since he died in 1955, his impact on the theology of the pre-conciliar decade was great, at least in his native country.

11. Yves Congar: *La Foi et la Théologie,* Paris, 1962.

For most of the essays that are now on the book-shelves of theological students were already available in periodicals where the knowledgeable reader could easily find them. Teilhard provided an eschatological orientation to theological work, a perspective in which theology did not appear to be splendidly isolated, but in which all sciences could again fulfill, though in a totally new way, their forgotten function of servants of theology. What Teilhard was doing for the science of nature, others would eventually do for contemporary philosophy and for the sciences of the mind.[12]

We could indefinitely continue this list of perspectives. Should we survey each theological specialization, we would run into the constant recurrence of similar phenomena. Though the field would be wide, a like pattern would prevail throughout. For, if the field is wide, all the questions are germane. The problems envisioned arose from one central point; the answers that were proposed and the attitudes that were adopted may be brought down to very few themes. Well-marked lines of thought crossed through the various problems and thus unified the answers. An Ariadne's thread ran through the manifold questions that were asked.

* * *

An opposition between "progressive" and "integralist" thinkers is often taken as basic to the pre-conciliar theological situation. And several accounts of the debates in Vatican II read the

12. The Teilhard de Chardin bibliography grows every day. His works have appeared in Paris since 1955.

speeches of the Council Fathers in the context of these categories. "Progressive" is easily understood. Yet it should be sharply distinguished from what was, and still is called in France "progressism." This is the movement connected with the ill-fated Montuclard. By "progressive" we simply mean theologians who are open to the modern world. As to "integralism," this word denotes a general attitude of faith that stresses self-defense and tends to consider offensive tactics the most suitable to defend the Church. This is often allied to a psychological complex of inferiority. In the theological field it opposes any sympathetic approach to all that is not the narrow system of scholastic theology, lest such an openness should spell danger to the Church.

This opposition of two tendencies explains many things in the conciliar controversies. Yet it should not be overstressed. Not all opposition to novelty came from integralists. Many a theologian who did not see eye to eye with the dominant figures of the theological scene such as Yves Congar and Henri de Lubac, could not be termed an integralist in any sense. The basic positions of theology are more dialectically related than this head-on clash between up-to-date and outmoded thinking.

There is a preliminary motive why a theologian will tend to progress or to stagnation. This underlying choice lies, I believe, in the following views of faith.

Faith is destined to be, as it were, incarnate in mankind; and the desire for faith is already inchoate in man's search for wisdom. This is a first standpoint from which theology may be viewed. But we may also see faith as essentially transcending man. It is revealed, coming from above as a free gift. By himself man can do nothing to acquire it. In the theology of faith these two points of view give rise to a choice between a *transcendental* or an *immanentist* emphasis. In the theology of the Church, this becomes an *eschatological* or an *incarnational* ecclesiology.

This seems to be at the core of contemporary theology.[13] Much of the theological fermentation since World War II arises from a dialectical exchange between, and a cross-fertilization of, both standpoints. Integralists are transcendentalists with an exclusive focus on apologetics and the defense of the faith. There are other manifestations of this "transcendentalism."

The *conservative* tendency does not go to the excesses of integralism. It does not restrict theology to polemics. On the contrary, it continues to build up the system of thought which the Catholic past duly tested. It correctly teaches that theology, being man's intellectual contemplation of the deposit of faith, looks to the past for its norms. Tradition is still living and growing, yet it is first of all embodied in the documents of the past. One of these is the philosophy and the theology of St. Thomas. As this is the most commonly accepted system, it becomes a norm of theological thought to the exclusion of non-Thomist scholasticism. By implication this attitude distrusts the philosophies that have grown outside of the Catholic past. The late Reginald Garrigou-Lagrange is a revered symbol of this side of theological controversies. Its dialectical opposite is the wide interest in the modern world shown by most French theologians.

The *speculative* tendency insists that theology is a systematic reflection, an intellectual contemplation. Its transcendent object requires a speculative approach if we are to apprehend it intelligently. This is "transcendentalism" again. It is primarily in-

13. Gustave Thils: *Théologie des Réalités Terrestres,* vol. 1, Paris, 1946, vol. 2, Paris, 1949; *Transcendence ou Incarnation? Essai sur la conception du christianisme,* Paris, 1950.

terested in the transcendent object of faith. Facing this, *positive* theologians are more concerned in tracing the historical development of dogma and the growth of theology as the human response to, the subjective apprehension of, the object.

These speculative theologians are not less well known or eminent than the positive theologians. Among the former we may mention M. T. Penido, Guérard des Lauriers, Cardinal Charles Journet, Garrigou-Lagrange and in general the motley group covered by the expression "the Thomists." Among the latter we find de Lubac, Daniélou, Dom Olivier Rousseau, for the Church Fathers; Chenu, Dom Jean Leclercq, Ephrem Longpré, Dom Odon Lottin, for the non- or pre-Thomist Middle Ages. Yves Congar seems to belong to a mixed type: he is an essentially speculative theologian who has methodically forced himself to minute historical investigations.

An excessively "transcendental" point of view increases the distance between theology and modern science. There are few theologians who are also scientists. Most enjoy only a second-hand acquaintance with the sciences. This is not usually a matter of principle. Many pure theologians are open toward science in general but have never had a chance to master any specific science. Yet it is possible to make a preliminary choice, not necessarily against science as such, but against its relevance to theological problems. This again arises out of a onesided stress on the transcendental aspect of theology, queen of knowledge, and therefore above the level of any purely human discipline.

A particularly acute opposition can be made between history, conceived as a science, and theology. Historical hypotheses, theories and interpretations vary. Faith does not. The transcendental-minded person is afraid lest faith should suffer from historical theories concerning, for instance, the origins of Christianity. That there have been conflicts is undeniable. That these conflicts should counsel a separation between theology and a historical method of research is another matter. The "incarnational" theologian wants to touch with his own hands the historical embodiment of faith and, accordingly, he does not shun history, but only bad historians. The "transcendentalist" prefers the supposedly safer path which more or less ignores historians.

Naturally enough, the classifications of real life are not as neat as they look on paper. The two sides, "incarnational-eschatological" or, in another perspective, "immanent-transcendental," have at times been somewhat blurred. The same man may stress one aspect of theology one day, and insist on another aspect when occasion calls for it. To give an instance, Guérard des Lauriers has appeared as a purely speculative theologian in his two magnificent volumes on faith;[14] as such we would list him among "transcendentalists." Yet he happens to be also a brilliant mathematician, a scientist-theologian, implicitly stressing "incarnation." Or consider the Oratorian Louis Bouyer: he cannot be called a conservative. Yet he could be catalogued under the label of "transcendency" on a number of issues. His essays on monastic spirituality definitely place him in the eschatological line of spirituality. In particular, unlike many French theologians, he has never delved into social problems. This may be considered a good pragmatic test of the "transcendental" mind. In any case, "incarnation" over against "transcendence" does not constitute a cut-and-dry category. Man, including the theological man, is too complex to be easily docketed. There may be alternances of several points of view in the same work. Thus Journet's *The*

14. *Dimensions de la Foi.* Paris, 1951.

Church of the Incarnate Word inserts historical developments in the speculative framework of Aristotelian causality. Or else it is sometimes doubtful whether an essay is speculative or positive: does a book on Thomism represent a genuine attempt at intellectual contemplation, a historical study of the thought of St. Thomas, or yet a mere rehash of the stunted Thomism of the class-room?

So far contemporary theology has been depicted in terms of attitudes, or trends. Two basic tendencies, incarnational and eschatological, dominate the scene. They inspire most, if not all, of the various options of Catholic theologians. Once more, however, a dialogue between two theologies should not harden into an opposition. Immanence and transcendence, being two aspects of God's relation to the world, are not exclusive. The incarnational and the transcendental standpoints in theology do not neutralize each other. I have used the term *dialectic* to describe this situation. It is a key to theology today. Where others would dread an antagonism, the Catholic mind thinks in terms of a mutual confrontation. This entails contrast, and also mutual fertilization. The union of points of view that would be exclusive in other provinces of thought, is a necessary condition of theological progress.

* * *

We should now survey some of the problems to which preconciliar theologians devoted attention. These will lead us straight to the theology of Vatican II. The problem of the nature of theology has already been singled out as being at the start of everything else at the present time and at the crossroads of several lines. We shall now prescind from this problem, though we shall never be far from it. Since a severe selection is imperious we will deal with both a historical question and a speculative one.

The works of recent theologians in patristics are well known. The wide success of the collection of texts, *Sources Chrétiennes,* and the popularity of a patrologist like Jean Daniélou, have advertised this interest in the Fathers, which has been emulated elsewhere, including America. It is significant, however, that none of the two American Catholic series of patristic texts (*Ancient Christian Writers* and *Fathers of the Church*) publishes its texts in the original language. And in the former only are translations accompanied by a commentary.

The main point I wish to illustrate now is not so well known, yet it is quite as important. There was a growing interest in the pre- and the non-Thomist Middle Ages. Before the last war there were remarkable studies on the 12th century: the works of Dom Lottin in ethics, those of J. de Ghellinck, S.J., the classic volume of G. Paré. Since the war the same topic has been brought to the fore again by de Ghellinck, Chenu and Dom Jean Leclercq, among others.[15]

A consistent picture emerges from those researches. We are beginning to know the Middle Ages before the 13th century, not as the vacuum it looks like if we are hypnotized by an isolated Thomism, but as a fascinating period for the theologian. It was

15. Odon Lottin: *Psychologie et Morale aux XIIe et XIIIe Siècles,* 4 vols., Paris, 1942–54; Jean de Ghellinck: *Le Mouvement Théologique au XIIe Siècle,* Paris, 1914; *L'Essor de la Littérature Latine au XIIe Siècle,* Paris, 1946; Gabriel Paré: *La Renaissance du XIIe Siècle,* Paris, 1933; Jean Leclercq: *L'Amour des Lettres et le Désir de Dieu. Initiation aux auteurs monastiques du moyen âge,* Paris, 1957, (ET: *The Love of Learning and The Desire for God,* New York, 1961); M. D. Chenu: *La Théologie au XIIe Siècle,* Paris, 1957.

the formative age of many scholastic tractates. Not only soteri-
ology, with St. Anselm; but also the sacramental synthesis, with
Hugh of St. Victor; the treatises on the virtues, the theology of
mysticism, with St. Bernard, William of St. Thierry, and the
Canons of St. Victor; the theological method with Abelard and
Peter Lombardus, made headway in the 17th century. We can now
look at the great schoolmen in perspective, as related to their
forerunners. And we realize that the 13th century held the 12th
in high esteem. As a token of this, I may refer to St. Bonaventure, saying that the Church Fathers are great in one or two
fields, but Hugh of St. Victor is first in all fields![16]

This is not all. Especially since Dom Leclercq and Father
Chenu have been at work, the Middle Ages are no longer the
age of scholasticism only. A distinction is made between the
theology of the schools, or scholasticism, and the theology of the
monasteries. Monastic theology flourished most in the 12th century. St. Anselm, St. Bernard, the Victorines, were monks. They
had a theology, and this was not scholastic. That is, it was not
destined to clerical students in search of learning, but to monks,
who were not interested in any formal study, but were motivated
by the monastic quest for God. Thus monastic theology does
not follow scholastic methods: the "question" is ignored. Like
scholasticism, it is essentially a commentary on Scripture. But
Holy Scripture is used, not as a source-book of theological insights, but as a dictionary of the spiritual life. The "anagogical"
sense of Scripture holds the light. Among the canonical books,
the Canticle of Canticles is most in favor: it tells the story of the
soul's relationship to God. Or at least so is it read by the monks.

16. *De Reductione Artium ad Theologiam*, n. 5.

On this groundwork there grows a meditative theology, what the older monks called *lectio divina, meditatio.*

The recovery of this original medieval theology, which was later superseded by scholasticism, carries important ecumenical consequences. The opposition between East and West, Eastern Orthodoxy and Western Scholasticism, largely disappears in it. Byzantine theology has never been scholastic; it is monastic. Western monastic theology features themes that also dominated Eastern monastic theology. For a part, this is because the sources of the Western monks were largely Eastern: the desert Fathers, Cassian, Origen. For another part, because monachism, whether it is lived in the East or in the West, requires the same fundamental attitudes of the soul in search of God.

A return, however partial, to this monastic theology would serve the ever recurring problem of unity between the Orthodox Churches and the Catholic Church.

Between this monastic theology and Thomism, modern studies have highlighted the fact that the theology of St. Bonaventure and of the first Franciscans belongs to both traditions. Scholastic by its methods, it remains monastic by its emphases.[17] At this point we may be reminded that when Pope Leo XIII launched the neo-scholastic revival, he did not envisage a purely Thomistic movement. Instead, he urged a return to both Thomas and Bonaventure, "those two lights shining in the house of God."[18] He thereby invited scholars to restore the monastic theology which is now coming back to light. Needless to say, however,

17. J. M. Bissen: *L'Exemplarisme Divin selon saint Bonaventure,* Paris, 1929; J. F. Bonnefoy: *Le Saint-Esprit et ses Dons selon saint Bonaventure,* Paris, 1929; G. Tavard: *Transiency and Permanence. The Nature of Theology according to St. Bonaventure,* 1954.

18. Leo XIII, letter *Quod Universa,* December 13, 1885.

this wish has not been fulfilled yet. The recovery of monastic theology should help fill a gap in modern Catholic culture.

We may call this survey to a temporary halt at this point, in order to see in what ways the theological problems that have been outlined found their way into the Vatican Council, and how they fared at the hands of the Council Fathers who, for the most part, were largely unacquainted with the theological fermentation of our times.

The Preparatory Theological Commission, as organized under John XXIII by Cardinal Alfredo Ottaviani, reflected the integralist point of view, united conservatism in method with a predilection for speculative rather than historical or biblical theology, and intended to stress the transcendental position of the Catholic faith and the Catholic Church over all human attitudes, efforts and achievements. To illustrate this convergence of several reactionary tendencies, Bishop Joseph De Smedt, coining a new word, denounced "triumphalism" in the Council.[19] To judge from the documents issued by this Commission, its purpose was not only to assert the rights of the Church and to man and equip the fortress of faith, but also to crush all other points of view hitherto accepted in the many mansions of the Catholic Church.

The story of the debates I will leave to others to tell. The uncertainty of the first few weeks, when the position of the majority of the Council remained undisclosed, was followed by violent verbal clashes, first over the liturgical reform, next over the question of Scripture and tradition. A majority appeared on the side of a reform following in the wake of the theological revival. And the minority was seen to defend positions still shared

19. December 1, 1962.

by the best minds in the Holy Office, but no longer in harmony with the more general opinions of theologians and the pastoral desires of most of the bishops. Thanks to Pope John's intervention on November 21, 1962, the majority was able to impose its point of view as the dominant one in the constitutions, decrees and declarations of the Council. Yet, largely due to the lull of the third session and to the concern of Pope Paul VI for unanimity in the Church, the fourth session was led to accept many of the criticisms coming from the minority, and to try to balance the documents so that justice would be done to all points of view. It is not the way in which this delicate balance was achieved that counts, however; it is rather the ultimate meaning and scope of the statements adopted and of the decisions finally made.

When the Council was being prepared, the main French theologians whose activities had been restricted under Pius XII were still under a cloud. Pope John had indeed quietly lifted the ban affecting some of the most influential ones; but they remained suspect to the officials of the Holy Office, who naturally could not see with great sympathy the uncoiling of the various measures which had been adopted to ensure the perenniality of scholastic theology and the continuation of the Counter-Reformation. For this reason, the names that hit the headlines most often during the Council sessions were not those of Congar or de Lubac, but those of German-speaking theologians from Germany, Austria or Switzerland, like Karl Rahner and Hans Küng. Yet the work done behind the scenes does not always correspond to the popular image of what is taking place. While Rahner and, to a lesser extent, Küng, had their influence, less well-known names from Germany were actually more important in the works of the Commissions. Much of the real work was done by those who were in a position to mediate between the advanced French and German thinkers and the slow-moving theologians used to more antiquated forms of thought. Several Belgians became masters at this difficult art: Philips, Charles Moehler, Gustave Thils, all from the University of Louvain, shared this task. It is, to a great extent, as a result of publicity that the reputations of Karl Rahner and Hans Küng, of the Flemish theologian Schillebeeckx, of the universities of Louvain and Nijmegen, of the Dutch bishops, are now higher in the Church at large than those of the true pioneers without whose prophetic work the Council could not have taken place.

It is not possible to summarize here the doctrinal formulations of the sixteen documents adopted by the Vatican Council, or even to indicate their main directions. As I have done it elsewhere for some of them,[20] there is no need to repeat it here. Far less is it possible to foresee their future sequels with certainty.[21] All I can do is to show how I understand the work done by the Council in general, without entering the details of the doctrinal exposés that the Council Fathers endorsed.

Some have spoken of the Vatican Council as "a new Pentecost."[22] This was even a favorite expression of John XXIII. Yet, in the Pope's speeches about the Council this could only be a hope—perhaps a prophecy—rather than the statement of an ascertained fact. Some, and myself among them, have spoken of "the end of the Counter-Reformation."[23] One may also speak of a passage from object to subject as the dominant preoccupation

20. *The Dogmatic Constitution on Divine Revelation,* Glen Rock, 1966.
21. *The Church Tomorrow,* New York, 1965.
22. *L. c.,* ch. 4
23. *L. c.,* ch. 2.

of theologians. There is little ground to quarrel with those appreciations of the historical importance of Vatican II in the development of Catholic theology. Yet, as the post-conciliar period advances, the need will be felt to assert continuity with the Counter-Reformation rather than discontinuity between the aftermath of Vatican II and that of Trent. For myself, now that the main theological "disputations" have taken place and that, by and large, the outcome has justified the theological movement of the 1940's, I would tend to rehabilitate the Counter-Reformation as a providential link between the great theology of the Middle Ages and that which may characterize, let us hope, the dawning 21st century.

In a recent survey of theology during the Council, in what he calls "the decisive decade," 1954–1964, Elmer O'Brien finds two phenomena as typical of contemporary thought. There is in the first place the appearance in Catholic thinking of something that has been rather frequent in Protestant circles: the development of "personal" theologies, that is, of "cohesive systems distinctively marked by the personalities of their authors."[24] O'Brien places the works of Henri de Lubac, Karl Rahner, Hans Urs von Balthasar, Jean Daniélou and John Courtney Murray in this category. I have difficulties with the fact that Yves Congar has been left out of the list, and with the statement that "the Murray theology is the most personal of any being produced these days by a Catholic scholar."[25] Yet, be that as it may, I am not so sure that this is a recent phenomenon. For, surely, the theologies of Johann Adam Möhler and of M. J. Scheeben in the 19th century do qualify as "personal" theologies.

24. *Theology in Transition,* p. 243.
25. *L. c.,* p. 246.

Elmer O'Brien adds, as generally applying to our period, the phenomenon of "the convergence of traditions."[26] Most of the theologians of our contemporary renewal have been, at one time or another, in one way or another, involved in the ecumenical movement. There has been a cross-fertilization of Catholic and Protestant thought, not only at the level of biblical scholarship, but also at that of theological reflection. This is indeed a remarkable progress on the attitude of former days, when Protestant theologies were hardly considered to belong among Christian theologies. But this is not simply the result of reading Protestant authors. It is in the first place the logical outcome of the advance of ecclesiological studies in Catholic theology.

Many have remarked on the absence of a formal treatise on the Church in scholastic *summae*. This treatise began its career in the 15th century, with the *De Ecclesia* of the Spanish Dominican John of Turrecremata. Later, the polemics of the Counter-Reformation oriented ecclesiological thought in an excessively apologetical direction. As a result, the proposed treatise was not fully developed. Only lately have theologians returned to the project. The works of Congar and Journet in this line are known to all.[27]

Unity has been traditionally studied as one of the four marks of the Church that are listed in the Creed. It should therefore belong to this treatise on the Church which is now in the making and to which Vatican II has contributed a chapter. Yet the back-

26. *L. c.,* p. 243.
27. Yves Congar: *Vraie et Fausse Réforme dans l'Eglise,* 2nd ed., Paris, 1957; *Jalons pour une Théologie du Laïcat,* Paris, 1953 (ET: *Lay People in the Church,* Westminster, 1956); Charles Journet: *L'Eglise du Verbe Incarné,* vol. 1, Paris, 1941; vol. 2, 1951, (ET of vol. 1: *The Church of the Word Incarnate,* New York, 1955); Jérôme Hamer: *The Church is a Communion,* New York, 1965.

ground of the problem has changed. Older theologians could easily start with the then obvious premise that the Church is one. They could trace back this unity, *structurally* to the episcopal organization of the Church under the primacy of the Bishop of Rome; *sacramentally* to the Real Presence in the Eucharist as the center of all Church life; *soteriologically* to the uniqueness of the Mystical Body of Christ as the realm of redemption; *doctrinally* to the oneness of the Catholic stream of tradition.

Contemporary Catholic theologians who study unity as a mark of the Church cannot overlook many things that could formerly be disregarded or that were simply inexistent. To the former unimpeachable standpoints, which have to be kept, they must add new points of view. *Ecclesiologically,* unity is fully shared nowhere, for the Catholic communion has suffered from the separations of the past that have lasted so long; furthermore, insofar as they share the faith and partake of the sacraments, separated Christians also participate, to an extent that may sometimes be hard to determine, in the unity of the Church. *Historically,* the institutional unity, which has been in the forefront of our theology since the Reformation, had been broken at the time of the Great Western Schism, when the Church did not agree on who was then the true Bishop of Rome: this raises many theoretical questions on the status of the papacy in the Church which are waiting for an answer or, even, for an acceptable formulation. *Ecumenically,* separated communities are achieving among themselves a degree of doctrinal unity or at least a Christian brotherhood: between this growing union and the Catholic unity, there must exist a connection that has to be carefully defined. *Psychologically,* unity is not only a quality of the collective body of the Church; there also is a spiritual and psychological

38

unity of individuals: and who can effectively call others to institutional unity if he is not fully unified himself? *Politically,* unity is also a world problem. *Scientifically,* the unity of a common formula covering all known phenomena has been envisaged; mankind, thanks to evolutionary theories, appears in closer unity with the cosmos than people could ever dream before.

These incidental lights cannot be neglected by theologians of Catholic unity. Authors like Congar, Bouyer, Bouillard, Journet, Thils, Karl Adam, Hans Urs von Balthasar, Jean Daniélou and scores of others have tried to assist the search for unity and thus, in the words of the Holy Office instruction *De motione oecumenica* (1949), to "promote" the ecumenical movement. Others have worked along connected or parallel lines. Thus the thought of Teilhard de Chardin may be viewed as a theology of cosmic unity within the framework of the Mystical Body.

All this shows that an old theological problem has been renewed in the light of the modern situation and of a better knowledge of the past. The polemics of the Reformation being now a memory, if an irksome one, theologians are better prepared than in the past to deal with the practical question: What can be done about Christian disunion? Many theoretical assertions can then be brought to bear on concrete issues with more relevance than could be done yesterday.

In this matter of the concrete application of theory to facts, contemporary theology has not been lagging. Researches in sacramental theology have influenced the liturgical movement; studies in missiology and in the notion of Catholicity have had results in the practice of Catholic Action or in home or foreign mission-work. However intellectually top-heavy it may seem to superficial onlookers, the renewal of the Church is actually plunged in burning problems of everyday apostolic life. However specialized and, even, sophisticated it may seem, theological work today is far from cut off from the life of the Church in general. This has been eloquently manifested in the concerns of the Vatican Council, which have been pastoral no less than theological.

* * *

It seems to me that all these lines converge on one characteristic. The "new Pentecost," the end of the Counter-Reformation, the multiplication of "personal" theological syntheses, the striving for the oneness of the Body of the Church, the pastoral concern for the workings of the Holy Spirit among the faithful: all these ideas suggest that our theology not only has been marked by the latent activity of the Holy Spirit; it is also being drawn toward a theology of the Spirit. Interest in the institutional Body of the Church has flowered into a closer focus on the Spirit in the Church. The impact of scientific exegesis on our reading of the letter of the Scriptures has given rise again to a search for their spiritual sense. Emphasis on liturgical rubrics has been replaced by a theology of liturgical participation, which is itself in the process of creating new and better forms of worship. The religious Orders are undergoing serious self-criticism in the light of a theology of the fundamental liberty of the Christian man and of a new look at the processes of Christian perfection. The promotion of the laity and the desire to give an effective voice to the feminine element in the Church reflect a deeper understanding of the "sense of the faithful" as one organ of the Spirit, and a more profound awareness of the feminine aspect of mankind in its relationship to Christ.

Thus, our thought in all areas is passing from the letter, from the body, from the external forms, from the institutions, from the routine, to a new sense of the Spirit, to a new conviction that Tradition is a living process, to a renewed faith that the body of Christ leads to his Spirit and that we would not be going anywhere unless we were drawn by the Spirit. That the Vatican Council has initiated a dialogue with all aspects of modern thought, from the most secular to the most religious non-Christian traditions, betokens the fact that we believe the Spirit to be at work in the universe at large in all the transformations of creation, from the slow-motion of paleontological ages to the sudden catastrophes of history, but especially in the long and slow meditation of all men of wisdom on the mystery of life.

II.

The Mystery of the Church

"THE MYSTERY of the Church" is the title of the first chapter of the constitution *Lumen Gentium,* in which the Second Vatican Council embodied its understanding of the Church.[1] What is meant by "mystery of the Church"? Obviously, this must be an important aspect of the Council's teaching, if it was deemed worthy to come first, and thus to introduce the entire topic. This emphasis, however, is far from new, since the notion of mystery has gained great importance in Catholic thought in the present century. At a philosophical level, the works of Gabriel Marcel and especially his Gifford Lectures for 1949 and 1950 on the *Mystery of Being*[2] have familiarized Catholic readers with a meaning of mystery rather different from that which people have in mind when they refer to some event as mysterious. A mystery is not, now, the incomprehensible or the suspect. It is an ontological quality profoundly embedded in being as category and

1. Translations have been published by NCWC (with discussion outline), by The Paulist Press (with Commentary by Gregory Baum), by Herder and Herder, in *The Documents of Vatican II,* by the Liturgical Press (with Latin Text). The Liturgical Press translation is the most accurate.
2. Gateway edition, 2 vols., Chicago, 1960.

as experience. The "ontological mystery" is being's demand for and appeal to transcendence. A mystery, in Marcel's own words, "can only be thought of as a sphere where the distinction between what is in me and what is before me loses its meaning and its initial validity."[3] In other words, a mystery is something in which I participate.

In the realm of liturgy and liturgical theology, the word *mystery* was reinterpreted by Odo Casel in reference to our participation in the death and resurrection of Christ.[4] "The" mystery is essentially our initiation—somehow on the remote type of the mystery-cults—to Christ's own mystery, namely his death and resurrection for the redemption of mankind. It has a theological aspect: the hiddenness of the divine Essence; an "economic" or soteriological aspect: the mission of Christ; a sacramental or liturgical aspect: the memorial of Christ's saving acts in the Church's worship, by which we are made present with Christ in his passage, through death and resurrection, to the Father.

Renewing with the medieval tradition of "mystery-plays," the liturgical revival of our times has focussed attention on the Christians' participation in the very acts of Christ, especially in the "paschal mystery," re-enacted by the Church during the great triduum of Holy Week.[5] The relationship of each eucharistic liturgy with Easter being otherwise self-evident, each liturgical celebration works what one author calls "the mystery par excellence, the one that alone the liturgy has to fulfil among us

3. *The Mystery of Being,* vol. I, p. 260.
4. Odo Casel: *The Mystery of Christian Worship,* (Westminster, 1962); Leo M. McMahon: "Towards a Theology of the Liturgy" (*Studia Liturgica,* vol. II, Winter 1964, n. 3, p. 129–154).
5. See Odo Casel: "Art und Sinn der Aeltesten Christlichen Ostfeier" (*Jahrbuch für Liturgie Wissenschaft,* Bd. 14, 1934).

at each moment of history"[6]: this is "the presence of the saving mystery," the presence among us of the Saviour Christ undergoing his passion, resurrection and ascension into heaven.

This liturgical concept of the mystery is central to the constitution of the Council on the liturgy, as instanced by the following passage:

At the Last Supper, on the night when he was betrayed, our Saviour instituted the Eucharistic sacrifice of his body and blood. He did this in order to perpetuate the sacrifice of the cross throughout the centuries until he should come again, and so to entrust to his beloved spouse, the Church, a memorial of his death and resurrection: a sacrament of love, a sign of unity, a bond of charity, a paschal banquet in which Christ is eaten, the mind is filled with grace, and a pledge of future glory is given to us.

The Church, therefore, earnestly desires that Christ's faithful, when present at this mystery of faith, should not be there as strangers or silent spectators; on the contrary, through a good understanding of the rites and prayers they should take part in the sacred action conscious of what they are doing, with devotion and full collaboration . . .

The constitution *De Ecclesia* also envisages the mystery and places it at the beginning of its consideration on the nature of the Church, as is suggested by the title of its first chapter, "The Mystery of the Church." What does the mystery mean when it is applied to the Church in the context of ecclesiological doctrine?

* * *

The word *mystery* itself appears only four times in the body of Chapter I; the related adjective *mystical* is used once in the expression *mystical body;* the adverb *mystically* also once, again in

6. Daniel Pézeril: "Le mystère pascal et l'homme d'aujourd'hui" (*La Maison-Dieu,* n. 68, 1961, p. 190).

relation to the Body of Christ. One of the uses of the word *mystery* can be disposed of quickly: it appears in the plural in reference to "the mysteries of Christ," by which one will easily understand the various aspects of the Church's doctrine concerning the Lord Incarnate. The other three passages containing the word *mystery* require closer attention.

In article 8 the following sentence serves as a conclusion to the entire chapter:

> By the power of the Risen Lord, she [the Church] is strengthened, that with patience and love she might overcome her sorrows and hardships, both internal and external, and reveal in the world the mystery [of the Lord], in shadows yet faithfully, until at the end it is manifested in full light.

The mystery, in this context, relates to Christ: it is the sum total of the revelation concerning the Lord, which the Church has the task of communicating to men. It cannot be fully grasped in this world and is known only darkly, as through a glass, in shadows. Yet it is the object of belief from which faith derives its certainty. On the basis of this quotation, the mystery of the Lord may be summed up in the Church's task of "announcing the cross and the death of the Lord until he come." The mystery which is the Gospel concerning the Saviour, is oriented to the past which it recapitulates, and to the future which it anticipates. The Church lives in the middle, at the present moment, as the meeting point of past and future, of the already acted *ephapax* of the cross and the still-to-come fulfillment of the return of Christ.

It is obviously in the light of the mystery of Christ that the mystery of the Church should be understood. The Council, however, does not simply speak of these two aspects of the Christian mystery. Between them, it places what it calls "the mystery of the Kingdom of God":

Christ, therefore, in order to fulfill the Father's will, inaugurated the Kingdom of the heavens on earth, revealed its mystery to us, and brought about redemption by his obedience. The Church, that is, the Kingdom of God already present in mystery, grows visibly in the world by the power of God.

Once again, the mystery is connected with revelation: it is that which is to be revealed. It is hidden in the bosom of God before revelation; it is then made known to us and we are initiated into it. The mystery is therefore the invisible presence on earth of the Kingdom of heaven as inaugurated by Christ in virtue of the redemption effected by his obedience. The presence of the Kingdom of God, or Kingdom of heaven, is no other than the Church, which, through its visible increase on earth, has the task of spreading the yet invisible Kingdom of God. It is a presence in mystery, in the hidden way of the cross; yet also, inseparably, in this very hiddenness as revealed in the Church's preaching. The invisible mystery is brought to men by the ministry of the Church, celebrating the Holy Eucharist and calling men to unity with Christ, thus proclaiming that Christ is the light of the world, the origin, the center and the end of all things.

As the channel of the mystery from God to the world, the Church is herself a mystery. In the words of article 5, "the mystery of the holy Church is manifested in its foundation. For the Lord Jesus marked the beginning of the Church by preaching the Good News, namely the coming of the Kingdom of God promised in the Scriptures for centuries . . ."

After showing the Kingdom in the Lord's words and miracles, the text relates this to the Church:

Therefore the Church, instructed by the gifts of her Founder and faithfully following his precepts of love, humility and self-sacrifice, receives the mission of announcing the Kingdom of Christ and of God

46

and of founding it in all nations; and she is herself on earth the seed and the beginning of this Kingdom.

In this luminous passage, the mystery of the Church is her close link with the Kingdom of God, which is also that of Christ: she preaches it and, so doing, implants it among those who receive her words with faith. As a result, the Church slowly spreads to the ends of the earth among all nations. The seed of the Kingdom is sown and it begins to grow and to bear fruits. For the Church's missionary function is oriented toward the final fulfillment of the Kingdom at the second coming of Christ; she is the germ and the beginning of the Kingdom. Her mystery is her preaching and her inchoative starting of the Kingdom.

This is related to the mystery of Christ, for the Kingdom is simply the realm of redemption and the triumph of Christ over evil and sin. It is the assumption of more and more people from more and more nations into the spiritual power of his death and resurrection, of what theology calls the *passa et acta Christi,* the passivities and the activities of Christ, his passion and his glorious deeds.

This understanding of the "mystery" is grounded in the doctrine of St. Paul, who described his own preaching as "the revelation of the mystery hidden in silence for eternity and manifested today" (Rom. 16:25). Similarly, the Council proclaims the revelation of the mystery: this is also the mystery of Christ, yet in as much as it includes the mystery of the Church.

* * *

An important aspect of the mystery of the Church may be perceived in the notably Trinitarian approach adopted by the constitution *Lumen Gentium.* Chapter I starts with a consideration of the benevolence of the Father, who desires to bring to-gether into one those who will believe in his Son—these being already chosen by the Father from all eternity, as his elect, "fore-known and predestined to be made conform to the image of his Son, that he may be first-born among many brothers." The Church of the Father, called by him through his Son and mani-fested in the Holy Spirit, stretches, in a well-known patristic view, "from Abel the just to the last of the elect" (art. 2).

The mystery unfolds itself in the mission of the Son sent by the Father, in whom the faithful have been chosen and pre-destined into adoption as sons before the constitution of the world. Through him the Church—the Kingdom of God in mystery—has been inaugurated; in him it will increase until the words of the Lord are fulfilled: "When I am exalted, I will draw all things to myself" (Jn. 12:32).

The panorama of the mystery continues to unfold itself in the function of the Holy Spirit, the Spirit of life, through whom the Father brings men to life after they have been dead through sin. He dwells in the Church and in the hearts of the faithful, guides her into all the truth, keeps her in unity and, by the power of the Gospel, renovates her for her final union with her Bride-groom, to whom "the Spirit and the Bride say, Come" (Apoc. 22:17).

Thus the mystery of the Church is essentially her hidden rela-tionship with the Father, the Son and the Spirit, which may be perceived by those who, being members of the Church, them-selves are involved in this relationship: they experience being called and elected by the Father, being drawn by the Spirit into adoption in the Son, being made mother, brother and sister to the Son.

This is summed up at the heart of Chapter I in a brief description of the Church as the Kingdom of God in mystery. This section was not in the first draughts of the schema presented to the Council for discussion, the text of which passed directly from a consideration of the Three Persons to the notion of the Mystical Body of Christ. A number of bishops, however, in the course of the debates, requested a treatment of the theme of the Kingdom of God, for this is a biblical theme and Jesus couched much of his teaching in the parables of the Kingdom. Some Council Fathers, however, objected that the New Testament does not identify the Church with the Kingdom of God: if the Church is a Kingdom, she is only the Kingdom of Christ, the Kingdom of God being purely an eschatological reality, not to be materialized in history. It is clear from the text as finally adopted that the Council took account of both suggestions. For it establishes no simple identity between the Church and the Kingdom. Their identity, as described here, is "in mystery." "The mystery of holy Church is manifested in her foundation . . ." The Church, following Christ, does not preach that she herself is the Kingdom pure and simple, but that the Kingdom comes in the words, the miracles and the presence of Christ. "Before all else," the text says, "the Kingdom is manifested in the person of Christ himself, the Son of man, who came to minister and to give his life a ransom for many." The heavenly Son of man of *Daniel* 7 and *10,* with whom Jesus identifies himself on several important occasions,[7] is now evoked; and this clearly indicates in what sense the Kingdom is understood. In the vision of Daniel, the Son of man receives the Kingdom: "To him was given dominion, honor

7. Oscar Cullmann: *Christology of the New Testament,* Philadelphia, 1959.

and kingdom, and all peoples, nations and tongues served him. His dominion is a dominion forever, which will not pass away, and his kingdom shall not be destroyed" (Dan. 7:14). Yet the same Kingdom is also given "to the people of the saints of the Most High" (7:27). It belongs to Christ, yet it also will be given to the elect. There is no suggestion that the Church constitutes, simply, today, the Kingdom of God. But it is affirmed that in her the Kingdom is coming. And this conviction urges the Church to a profound desire toward the total manifestation of the Kingdom: "Meanwhile, while she increases little by little, she aspires after the consummation of the Kingdom, and with all her strength she hopes and desires to be united with her King in glory."

In the meantime, before this consummation is fulfilled, the Church's activities, entirely oriented toward the Kingdom, consist in "announcing the Kingdom of Christ and of God, and in founding it in all the nations." In other words, the Church can only be "the seed and the beginning": her center waits ahead of her, in the full Kingdom. In her present state, she is not an ultimate reality, but she looks forward to and she heralds the ultimate reality of the Kingdom of God.

The evanescent character of the Church on earth appears with striking clarity in the New Testament. For this reason, the constitution devotes considerable space to the scriptural images under which the Church is symbolically described. These are grouped together according to types, and come in the following order: the fold and the flock; the field and the vine; the building, the house of God, the family, the dwelling, the tent, the Temple, the holy City; finally, the bride of the Lamb. This leads to a special treatment of the image, more familiar to Catholics of our generations, of the Body of Christ (art. 7).

The gradation of these scriptural symbols should be noticed.

As the text says at the beginning of Article 6, "Just as in the Old Testament the revelation of the Kingdom is often proposed in symbols, today likewise the inner nature of the Church is made known to us through various images . . ."—whose purpose is to lead us step by step from a more superficial to a deeper understanding of the Church. This progression may be seen in that the images are borrowed from more and more human types of realities: the field, the house, the bride, the Body. The *field* is exterior to man, even though the farmer knows it intimately from working in it. The *house* is closer to him, since it is man's dwelling place and it is made by him. The *bride* corresponds to a further degree of intimacy, for she is much closer to man than the house which shelters them. The *Body* represents the ultimate in immediate experience. Thus, even apart from the scriptural meaning of these images, their selection and gradation betrays a desire to bring the understanding of the Church as near to experience as possible. Their meaning will therefore be: The Church is to God and Christ what his flock is to a shepherd, his field to a farmer, his home to any man, his wife to her husband, his body to a human being. For each of these images and others connected with them, the Council points out its relevance to God and to the work of Christ in the Church. Thus, Christ is the gate leading to the fold; God is the shepherd and the husbandman; Christ is the Vine, the angular stone on which the Church is built, the one who loved the Church, his Bride, and united her to himself in love and fidelity. Such a gradual approach embeds the mystery of the Church in a profoundly Christological context.

A prominent place is also given here to the Old Testament. This is not unusual, for Catholic doctrine has always stressed both the continuity and the discontinuity of the Old and the New

Testaments. Yet it has not always, at least in its popular accounts, given much importance to the Old Testament in the theology of the Church. However, the line of thought adopted in this chapter follows the patristic idea of the continuity of divine election "from Abel the just to the last of the elect." In the same perspective, the Church was "foreshadowed from the origin of the world . . . marvelously prepared in the history of the People of Israel and in the Old Covenant." Although the Church as such is only "constituted in the last days," that is, at the coming of Christ, the just of the Old Covenant belong to her and will be gathered in the New Jerusalem (art. 2).

The Old Testament roots of the scriptural images of the Kingdom are therefore seen to be constitutive of their meaning and relevance. The image of the flock and the shepherd refers us to Isaiah, Ezekiel, Zechariah. The vine is a well-attested prophetic image. The comparisons of the tent and of the Temple would be meaningless without the rich Old Testament background concerning them and the liturgical experiences of the Jews.[8] The New Jerusalem must be understood in the perspective of the spiritual meaning of the Old Jerusalem, the City of Peace on Mount Zion. This ultimately implies, for Christian ecclesiology, the seriousness of the Covenant passed with our Father Abraham and recapitulated in Christ, the graciousness of the election by which we have been called to belong to the Assembly of the predestined, the earnestness of a call which does not proceed from anybody's previous merits but from the loving initiative of the Father, who chose the faithful in Christ before the foundation of the world. Thus all ecclesiological Pelagianisms and Semi-Pelagianisms are rendered unthinkable and impossible.

8. Yves Congar: *Le Mystère du Temple,* Paris, 1958, (ET: *The Mystery of the Temple,* Westminster, 1962).

The description of the Church in terms of its scriptural symbols is climaxed by a long passage on the image of the Body of Christ. Theological reflection on the Body of Christ has been extremely important in the Catholic ecclesiology of the last decades. Contrary to what some authors seem to think, Catholic ecclesiology today is not, and has not been for a long time, an ecclesiology of the Institution. On the contrary, there is considerable truth in the following remark made in a recent survey of Catholic theology in France: "The mystery of the Church has become for many, if not for most of the contemporary theologians, the touchstone of their thought and work."[9] This could be seen in one of the major tools in the renewal of Catholic theology, the series of volumes of the French collection *Unam Sanctam*, which is devoted to ecclesiology. It could also be shown by a survey of the most significant theological authors of the last three decades. The theology of the Mystical Body has had a wide seminal influence since the pioneer studies of Emile Mersch.[10] This movement was crowned in 1943 by Pius XII's encyclical, *Mystici Corporis*, and by Henri de Lubac's outstanding study, *Corpus Mysticum*.[11] That these publications took place during the war years may have hidden their significance to those who were not directly involved in Catholic theological work. Yet there can be little doubt that much of the constitution *Lumen Gentium* and much of the work of the Council in general, derive from their impetus.

The encyclical *Mystici Corporis* developed the idea of the Church as the Body of Christ mainly from the standpoint of the

9. James Connolly: *The Voices of France*, p. 96.
10. *The Theology of the Mystical Body*, St. Louis, 1951. See also Gustave Weigel: *Catholic Theology in Dialogue* (New York, 1960), ch. 1: "Catholic Ecclesiology in Our Times."
11. Paris, 1944.

53

organic unity of a body, thus finding it appropriate to describe the wonderful organic unity of Christ and his Body, the Church. Christ stands at the head of his Body the Church. This does not imply that he would be other than the Body, but that He has the pre-eminence of the Head over the other members, and that the influx of life passes from the Head into the Body. The Church and Christ constitute, in the words of the encyclical, *Christus totus,* the total Christ: this is the Christ of Palestine, yet extending his influence to all those who, by faith, by the sacraments and by communion with the chief organs of the body, are included in the Church. At the same time, the symbol of the Body is completed, in the encyclical, by that of the soul in the body, which is identified with the Holy Spirit. It is significant of the mentality of this encyclical, however, that, whereas the notion of Body is fairly adequately investigated and explained, that of "mystery" and of the related adjective *mystical* is definitely "dated" and, all things considered, slightly deficient: mystical is contradistinguished from physical on the one hand and moral on the other. It is of another order than the physical and is of more reality than a merely moral unity or conjunction. Mystical, then, connotes the action of the Holy Spirit as giving life and substance to the Body. The mystery, however, is not seen in the Pauline line of thought, as that which is hidden is God and now finally revealed, into which the faithful are initiated by the sacraments of faith; it seems rather to be taken in the sense of something beyond comprehension, unfathomable. Thus the encyclical calls the dwelling of the Holy Spirit in the soul, which accounts for the cohesion of the Mystical Body, an "occult mystery."

These brief remarks may enable us to grasp the scope of the constitution *Lumen Gentium* in its treatment of the Body-image.

As presented here, the image of the Church as the Body of Christ is radically soteriological, its treatment being based on a consideration of the salvific function of Christ: "In the human nature united to himself, the Son of God, overcoming death by his own death and resurrection, redeemed man and transformed him into a new creature. Sharing his Spirit, he mystically made his brothers, gathered from all nations, into his own body." The use of the adverb *mystically,* rather than of the adjective *mystical,* adds another dimension to the doctrine of the Body of Christ, in so far as it points out the way in which the Body is constituted. That it is formed "mystically" implies, in the Pauline and traditional identification of mystery and sacrament, of mystical and sacramental, that the many faithful are made one Body in a sacramental action. The Body of Christ, mystically constituted out of many believers gathered into one, is not a previous entity which one is invited to join. Rather it is created by the very sacraments of introduction into Christianity, so that the mystery of Christian initiation is at the same time and by the same token the mystery of the creation and increase of the Body of Christ.

For this reason the Council continues with a short survey of the contribution of Baptism and the breaking of the Bread to the structure of the Body of Christ, which leads it to affirm both the unity and the diversity of the Body. For the many who are made one do not thereby lose their proper functions and inspirations. One and the same Body needs many organs and many charisms. The text makes a distinction between the functions—and especially that of apostleship, which is alone specifically mentioned at this point—and the charisms of the faithful. All contribute to the upbuilding of the Body of Christ and proceed from

the same Spirit; "yet the Spirit himself made the charisms sub-
servient to the authority" of the apostles. In other words, no one
may argue from charismatic gifts or prophetic callings against
the apostolic function. There can be no contradiction between
structural functions and personal inspirations, for the Spirit never
contradicts himself. The link between functions and charisms,
especially when a conflict seems to be in the making, is preserved and guaranteed by the love communicated to all by the
Spirit, "so that, if one member suffers, all members suffer; if
one member is honored, all members rejoice."

Unity and diversity in the Body have the function of extolling
and serving the primacy of Christ, the Head, over all men and
all things in the Church and in the universe. Although the
primacy belongs to Christ in His Eternity as "the image of the
invisible God," it also attaches to him as "the first-born from
among the dead." His oneness with the faithful reaches as far
as a conformity, as the sharing of the same form through the
believer's assimilation to what our text calls the "mysteries of
the life" of Christ, a classical expression of Catholic Christology
and spirituality, which the text relates to St. Paul. Conformity
entails imitation of Christ in his passivities, so that we may be
united to him also in his glorification.

Following still the Pauline development of the image of the
Body, our text speaks next of the increase of the Body under the
influx of the Head, in such a way that the Head no longer functions as the chief member, but as that toward which the Body
grows: ". . . doing the truth in love, we increase in all things in
him who is our Head." This is the fruit of the Holy Spirit. In a
more guarded language than that of the encyclical *Mystici Corporis,* the Council asserts that the Spirit's function "could be
compared by the holy Fathers to the function of the principle

of life or soul in the human body." Clearly, this cannot be a totally adequate comparison and an analogy in the strict sense. For the soul and the body, in Aristotelian philosophy, are interdependent, whereas the Body of Christ which is the Church is subordinated to the Spirit, whose immanence in the Church never diminishes his Transcendence.

This treatment of the image of the Body of Christ concludes with a return to that of the Bride.[12] This is again a Pauline feature, since the two images also come together in St. Paul. "Christ loves the Church as his Bride." The Pauline notion of the *pleroma,* of the Church as the fullness of Christ, ends this section on an eschatological note. The Church, which is the Body and the fullness of Christ, still has to "reach all the fullness of God." In other words, our initiation into the Body will not be over until the Church has attained to her total growth, when the fullness of Christ on earth equates the fullness of God in heaven. The image of the Body of Christ as applied to the Church is thus essentially dynamic, turned toward the final fulfillment of all things in the line and on the prolongation of the sacraments of Christian initiation, by which we are mystically made into the Body of Christ growing through time and space.

* * *

That the Church is the Body of Christ, his Bride, his Flock, the anticipation of the Kingdom of God, and whatever else the scriptural metaphors indicate, means something very real to Catholic theology. The dichotomy introduced in the Reformation and already in late medieval theology, between the concrete,

12. On the Church as "bride," see Daniel Berrigan: *The Bride. Essays in the Church,* New York, 1959; Karl Delahaye: *Ecclesia Mater chez les Pères des Trois Premiers Siècles,* Paris, 1964.

empirical Church and the Church of the elect, which is the Body of Christ, would have been unthinkable for the Church Fathers, who did not work within the framework of a universe conceptually divided into matter and spirit. Biblical thought did not separate the concrete community and the Chosen People, any more than body and soul in man. On the contrary, the integral unity of man as "flesh," once it is applied to the Holy Community, makes it inseparably earthly and heavenly, material and spiritual. Duality between an empirical and a spiritual Church appeared in various medieval sects, but did not gain respectability until the Reformation, in some at least of its forms, accepted it. For the continuing Catholic understanding of the Church, however, this duality has been, and remains today, inexistent.

This is the background for the last section of Chapter I of the constitution, in which the Church is called "the community of faith, hope and love," and described in its two parallel aspects: "The society structured with hierarchical organs and the Mystical Body of Christ, the visible assembly and the spiritual community, the earthly Church and the Church endowed with heavenly goods, must not be considered as two things, but constitute a single complex reality rooted in a divine and a human element." The Catholic faith asserts the unity of these elements, yet adheres to no specific theory as to the manner of their unity. An analogy, proposed in the constitution, compares the unity of the divine and the human in the Church to their unity in Christ: "As the assumed nature serves the divine Word to whom it is inseparably united as the living organ of salvation, so, in a way which is not dissimilar, the social organism of the Church serves the Spirit of Christ who vivifies it for the building up of the Body." The analogy is proposed with care: it is called "a non-mediocre analogy," and it is said to be "not dissimilar," expressions that are not as forceful as straight affirmative ones would be. This is obviously intended to avoid too univocal an understanding of the comparison. For while the human aspects of the incarnation and of the Church correspond, the divine aspects do not: the Church cannot be divine in the same way as the Incarnate Lord is. By adopting the analogy with caution, the Council endorsed to some extent a current of Catholic ecclesiology which has made considerable use of it, pointing out that both ecclesiological Monophysitism and ecclesiological Nestorianism break the unity of the spiritual and visible Church, and opposing Protestant ecclesiologies on the basis of the faith in the incarnation as defined at the Council of Chalcedon.

It remains that this analogy points to the nature of the unity of the visible and the spiritual: the visible is at the service of the spiritual, and is its instrument for the salvation of mankind, as the humanity of Christ is the instrument of his divinity and, in Thomistic terms, the "instrumental cause" of salvation. Because a Council should not normally enter philosophical and theological debates, the text makes no mention of instrumental causality. Indirectly, however, the theology which sees the relationships between the visible and the spiritual in the Church, between the Catholic institution and the Mystical Body, on the type of instrumental causality is bound to come reinforced from meditating on this passage of the constitution *De Ecclesia*. The instrumental causality in question obtains, in Thomism, between the humanity and the divinity of Christ, between the visible and the spiritual elements in the sacraments, between the visible and the spiritual aspects of the Church. In other words, we are indirectly invited to understand the dialectic of the visible and the invisible in the framework of sacramental theology.[13]

If one should ask for a more dynamic expression of this relationship, a short passage from the Constitution on the Liturgy may help us to complete the perspective:

> It is of the essence of the Church that she be both human and divine, visible, yet invisibly equipped, eager to act yet intent on contemplation, present in this world and yet not at home in it; and she is all these things in such wise that in her the human is directed and subordinated to the divine, the visible to the invisible, action to contemplation, and the present world to that city yet to come which we seek." [art. 2]

The two elements or aspects which the Constitution on the Church correlates on the pattern of the human and the divine in Christ, appear now in terms of orientation and intentionality: the Institution is oriented toward the heavenly Kingdom, so that all its elements promote the Kingdom and aspire to it with eager longing.

The problem of the unicity of the Church immediately follows the assertion of the identity of the empirical, visible Church with the spiritual community of the elect. There can only be one communion on earth of those whom the Father has introduced into the fellowship of his Incarnate Son. Hence the following paragraph:

> This is the one Church of Christ, which in the Creed we confess to be one, holy, catholic and apostolic, which our Savior after his resurrection entrusted to Peter to shepherd, and to the other apostles also to spread and to rule, and which he built up as the column and the foundation of truth for ever. This Church subsists as a constituted and organized society in this world in the Catholic Church governed by the successor of Peter and the bishops in communion with him . . .

13. For a discussion of this question, see Jérôme Hamer: *The Church is a Communion*, pp. 87–100, with the footnote on Karl Rahner, p. 95.

The ecumenical fellowship of all Christians presents the one danger that the problems that divide them may appear at times out of focus. Various reports, which followed the third session of the Council, expressed the dismay of some Protestant authors at the fact that, whereas the Council did seem prepared to make many practical changes, it was in no mood to alter basic doctrines, like the belief in the primacy of Peter and of his successors the bishops of Rome.[14] In view of the nature of faith, any such expectation would of course be naïve; and the solution to Christian disunion cannot consist in abandoning the claims of truth in deference to love. It was therefore essential for the Council to teach the full Catholic belief concerning the nature of the Church. It is, for the Second Vatican Council, an integral part of the mystery of the Church, hidden in the designs of God, revealed through his Son and, as we also believe, manifested through the providential march of history, that the one Church which is on earth the herald of the Kingdom of God should have a visible, social aspect inseparable from its invisible, spiritual one, and identical with the organism of the Catholic Church under the bishops in communion with the Bishop of Rome. As this introduces the concept of the hierarchy, I will deal with it at greater length in relation with the third chapter of the constitution.

The identification of the Catholic organism with the visible aspect of the one, holy, catholic and apostolic Church should not be understood as arrogance. On the contrary, it implies the desire of the visible Church to be one with her Lord in his humility.

14. One may find reflections on the belief that "the papacy" remains "the main obstacle to reunion" in Frederick C. Grant: *Rome and Reunion*, New York, 1965. Grant was for some time one of the Anglican observers at the Vatican Council.

At this point one may feel the hand of the many bishops who, during the Council sessions, expressed a wish to see the Church as "the Church of the poor," identified with the poor and the persecuted throughout the world. For the Lord, "though he was in the form of God, emptied himself, receiving the form of the servant" (Phil. 2:6). In her passivities much more than in the external pageant of her ceremonies and in the glory of her "princes," the Church becomes similar to her Lord. She therefore acknowledges him "in the poor and the suffering." The Church also knows that she is a mixed community, counting sinners as her members, and she therefore continuously "pursues penance and renovation." One should not read into this, however, the notion that the Church may be at the same time "holy and sinful" on the pattern of Luther's understanding of the justification of the sinner.[15] The Church is not *simul justa et peccatrix,* but, in the words of the constitution, *sancta simul et semper purificanda,* "holy and always, at the same time, to be purified." Holiness is inseparable from the spiritual status of the Church as the realm of redemption, as the herald of the New Jerusalem, as the beginning of the Kingdom of God. Yet, purification belongs to her visible, earthly aspect, which stands always in need of greater conformity to the image of her Lord.

* * *

This survey of the mystery of the Church may end here, although some of the points made in it will be clarified in the

15. On this point, see *The Church Tomorrow,* pp. 50–56. The theme of the mystery of the Church at the Vatican Council is studied by Cardinal Charles Journet: "Le mystère de l'Eglise selon le deuxième Concile du Vatican" (*Revue Thomiste,* janvier–mars 1965, pp. 5–51).

course of the following pages. We should remember, at the end as at the start, that the mystery, in the language of the Council, is now being revealed. Hidden and secret, it is presented to men, that they may enter into it with faith and thereby obtain light and life. The mystery of the Church is the way in which the Kingdom of God is now in process of formation. And the mystery of the Kingdom is the progressive manifestation of the Lord, to whom "dominion, honor and kingdom" have already been given.

In its hiddenness, the mystery may seem like "scandal to Jews and foolishness to Gentiles"; to those, however, to whom it is revealed, it is "the wisdom of God and the power of God" (1 Cor. 1:23–24). By placing its ecclesiology in the light of the "mystical" event at the core of the Christian faith, —the revelation of the Kingdom of God in Christ—, the Vatican Council has opened new avenues to theology. It has renewed with a traditional theme widely exploited by the Fathers and deeply rooted in the Scriptures. By so doing, it has made it possible to think of the Church in terms that are less scholastic, less Latin and less Western than we have been used to. The ecclesiology of the Council contains the germ of a more Semitic, therefore a more integral and a more "catholic," approach to the problems of the Church than has characterized Catholic thought since the beginning of the Counter-Reformation.

III.

The People of God

SOME OF THE major speeches of the second session of the Council
were occasioned by the treatment of the notion of People of God
in the proposed schema or draft, *De Ecclesia*. Briefly, the schema
followed this order: the mystery of the Church; the hierarchy and
especially the episcopate; the People of God and especially the
laity; the call to holiness in the Church. These four chapters constituted an incomparable improvement upon the very first draft,
prepared by the Preliminary Theological Commission. Nonetheless, as was pointed out by many bishops, it presented the anomaly
of placing the hierarchy between the Mystery of the Church and
the People of God. It was of course never the intention of the
Commission to separate the hierarchy from the People; yet the
resulting ecclesiology juxtaposed functions and status instead of
organically relating them to each other within the oneness of
the Church. The revision that was then made purposed to stress
the organic character of the Church, in which all "orders" are,
like the members of a body, at the service of one another. The
central problem concerned the hierarchy, and specifically the re-

lations of bishops, individually and collegially, with the Pope's primacy over the universal Church. Yet the Council could not be satisfied with elucidating the place and task of bishops. Considerable attention was brought to bear, in the last few decades, on the laity and its place in the Church. This had to be taken account of, lest the laity be greatly disappointed. As Pope Paul stated in the address by which he opened the second session,

It will be necessary to elucidate the teaching regarding the different components of the visible and mystical body, the pilgrim, militant Church on earth, that is, priests, religious, the faithful, and also the separated brethren who are called to adhere to it more fully and completely.

How this is done in the constitution as promulgated may be briefly explained: after describing the Church as the People of God, the constitution elaborates on the hierarchy, the laity, the members of religious Orders. The only "orders" that do not receive full treatment are that of the priesthood and the related order of the diaconate.

* * *

The Protestant circles that pay great attention to Covenant theology may be gratified to know that the Council's treatment of the theme "People of God" begins with a little piece of Covenant theology:

At all times and in every race God has given welcome to whosoever fears him and does what is right. God, however, does not make men holy and save them merely as individuals, without bond or link between one another. Rather has it pleased him to bring men together as one People, a People which acknowledges him in truth and serves him in holiness. He therefore chose the race of Israel as a People unto himself. [art. 9]

These beginning lines point out the major difference between a Protestant Covenant theology and what the Council wishes to say. For the following definition of a Covenant by Herman Witsius (1636–1708) does not tally with what the Council calls a Covenant:

A Covenant of God with man is an agreement between God and man about the method of obtaining consummate happiness, with the addition of a threatening of eternal destruction, with which the despiser of the happiness offered in that way is to be punished.[1]

In the constitution De Ecclesia, a Covenant is essentially collective: it is creative of the "messianic people," namely "Israel according to the flesh," already called the "Church of God," that is, the Cahal Yahweh, and, after the coming of Christ, the "New Israel, which, while living in this age, goes in search of a future and abiding city," and which "is called the Church of Christ" (art. 9). The Covenant is not with a man or with a multitude of men; it does not concern individuals directly, but a People, Israel, the Church, " a visible and social union," "a communion of life, charity and truth." To the Old People of God, the race of Israel, the New People of God has succeeded, made up of Jew and Gentile, united "not according to the flesh but according to the Spirit."[2]

Evidently, this People comprises individuals: these are "those who believe in Christ, who are reborn not from a perishable but from an imperishable seed through the word of the living God,

1. Herman Witsius: Of the Covenants, vol. 1, ch. 1, n. ix (Edinburgh, 1791, vol. 1, p. 57).
2. On the theology of the People of God, see Congar: Lay People in the Church, Westminster, 1957; George Tavard: The People of God, Glen Rock, 1965; Anscar Vonier: The People of God, New York, 1937; Charles Journet: L'Eglise du Verbe Incarné, vol. II.

not from flesh but from water and the Holy Spirit"; they are "all those who in faith look upon Jesus as the author of salvation and the source of unity and peace." The stress, however, lies on their unity and cohesiveness, not on their individuality and separateness. For they are "gathered together as one"; they are "established as the Church" which "transcends all limits of time and confines of race," and which is, in the words of 1 Peter 2:9-10, "a chosen race, a royal priesthood, a holy nation, a purchased people . . . who in times past were not a people but are now the People of God."

The Old Testament has seen the Saviour as a "Royal Priest," a King who would be Priest and a Priest who would be King, comparable to Melchizedek or David. In the Messiah priesthood and kingship would be one. Royal Priesthood was an attribute of the Saviour.

The use of this messianic title implies that Christians should manifest the royal priesthood of Christ in themselves. They do this by simply being faithful, by "coming to him as to a living stone." His messiahship is to shine through us, not so much in what we do as in what we are. To live with Christ and let him shape us as he wishes is to share in his messiahship or royal priesthood. But priesthood is a liturgical function. In his high-priestly function, Christ saves his disciples by including them in the eternal offering of the *Logos* to the Father. Christ as the Royal Priest cannot therefore be disassociated from those in whom his priesthood is at work. In a very profound sense, Christians are the royal priesthood of Christ: they are what can be seen of it on earth. The Messiah was seen by the apostles. Today, however, men can know him only through his presence among the Christian People, in that they love one another. It is through today's People of God that Christ approaches our contemporaries as their Messiah, their Royal Priest, their Saviour. This defines the *being* of the People of God: "The baptized, by regeneration and the annointing of the Holy Spirit, are consecrated as a spiritual house and a holy priesthood . . ." (art. 10).

This emphasis on *being* the People of God introduces a complementary emphasis on *behaving* as the People of God "in order that through all those works which are those of the Christian man they may offer spiritual sacrifices, and proclaim the power of him who has called them out of darkness into his marvelous light" (art. 10).

A people, a nation or a race, is a group of men and women who live and die, who work and rest, who eat and drink, who build, who love, who bear children, who are happy and unhappy. To be a people means to live side by side within one tradition. It implies sharing a common past out of which we look forward to a common future. As a race, a nation and a people, the faithful are indistinguishable from others but for one thing. Their daily actions are those of everyone around them. They are not set apart in the sense of having escaped the usual conditions of existence. They should not be know from their habits, their customs or their art. Their center is not a folklore, a culture or a history but a *faith*. What distinguishes the People of the faithful is their faith, the fact—so simple and yet so incomprehensible—that alone in the universe they know that the mystery of life and death was manifested on earth, on a hill near Jerusalem, when the author of life was put to death. They know that this manifestation was completed in a nearby cave, when the Lord Jesus, having tasted death, triumphed over it. The Church is the People that lives in the hope of sharing this triumph. Out of its past, known by faith, it looks to the future with hope, and it lives the present with love.

This spiritual status of the People of God, which defines its common priesthood, is intimately connected with the sacraments of the Catholic tradition, of which the Council speaks in article 11.

Baptism marks the start of the common priesthood.[3] It associates the faithful to the death and resurrection of Christ, includes them in the predestined number of those who are reached by salvation and elected by the Saviour as channels of his messianic priesthood. "Reborn as sons of God, they must confess before men the faith which they have received from God through the Church."

Confirmation is connected with the active presence of the Holy Spirit: "The Holy Spirit endows them with special strength, so that they are more strictly obliged to spread and defend the faith, both by word and by deed, as true witnesses of Christ." In the next section, article 12, this witness is presented as a "share in Christ's prophetic office." For the Spirit is the "seal" of the Holy Trinity. Confirmation, traditionally conferred through a "sealing," with *chrism,* of the Christ-like character acquired in Baptism, gives a share of the Spirit. It mysteriously makes a man or a woman of this century one of the disciples gathered in the Upper Room, "when the day of Pentecost had come" (Acts 2:1). It marks the renewal of the Pentecostal life.

At this point we may be in danger of mistaking the antics of emotional revivals with the urge of the Spirit, an upsurge

3. On the common priesthood of the faithful, see Paul Dabin: *Le Sacerdoce Royal des Fidèles,* 2 vols., Bruges, 1941–50; Bishop Emile Joseph De Smedt, *The Priesthood of the Faithful,* Glen Rock, 1961.

from our subconscious depths with the Pentecostal "mighty wind." In Genesis creation was chaotic *before* the "Spirit of Yahweh moved over the surface of the waters." (Gen. 1:2) *After* the Spirit had come, there is, with more abundant life, knowledge of all truth. Knowledge implies orderliness. The witnessing life of a confirmed Christian follows an order and is set in a framework. The life in the Spirit is a synthesis of contemplation and action. It is neither the former without the latter, for true contemplation issues into action, nor the latter apart from the former, for action is worth what contemplation makes it. The Pentecostal share of the Holy Spirit, sacramentally granted in Confirmation, is a fountainhead of peace and harmony. It gives "charisms," some of which are "extraordinary gifts," whereas others are "more simple and widely diffused." Above all, it protects the unanimity of the faithful by giving them what the Council calls, after a traditional expression, *sensus fidei,* the "sense of the faith" by which, "anointed as they are by the Holy One, they cannot err in faith." The charismatic functions in the People of God formed the topic of a conciliar speech of Cardinal Léon Joseph Suenens, who asked that "the importance of prophets and teachers in the Church be given attention."[4] This passage of the constitution crowns a movement which was given impetus by Cardinal John Henry Newman's essay in *The Rambler* of July 1859, "On Consulting the Faithful in Matters of Doctrine,"[5] and the theology of which reached its climax in Congar's long chapter on "The Laity and the Prophetic Function of the Church," in his *Jalons pour une Théologie du Laïcat*

4. Daniel O'Hanlon (ed.): *Council Speeches of Vatican II,* Glen Rock, 1964, p. 34.
5. Reprinted in *Cross Currents,* Summer 1952, pp. 69–97.

(1953).[6] The endorsement of the *sensus fidelium* by the Ecumenical Council was, moreover, prepared by the actions of the last Popes in the matter of "promoting the laity," notably by Pius XI's creation of "Catholic action" as "a participation of the faithful in the hierarchic apostolate," and by Pius XII's endorsement of the "world congresses for the apostolate of the laity" and the remarkable addresses that he pronounced on these occasions.

The "sense of the faithful" is equally shared by laymen and members of the hierarchy. It is not a prerogative of the laity, but belongs to all orders and functions, insofar as they are rooted in the People of God. It therefore implies an organic relationship of the diverse orders, which is manifested in "the universal consensus in matters of faith and morals, from the bishops to the outmost ring of the lay faithful" (art. 12), as the Council says, borrowing an expression from St. Augustine. The result is the inclusion of all believers into a People with one mind and one soul: "Through it, the People of God adheres unwaveringly to the faith given once for all to the saints, penetrates it more deeply with right judgement, and applies it more fully in life" (art. 12).

The sacrament of the Holy Eucharist occupies a special place among the constitutive elements of the People of God.[7] Baptismal grace, reinforced and completed by Confirmation, revives day after day, not through our works and merits, but through God's sacramental action. To receive the body and blood of Christ is to

6. English translation: *Lay People in the Church,* 1957. The time-lag between the original publication and the American translation of French and German theological studies is sometimes considerable, so that the American cultured public is not always up to date. The discovery of Pierre Teilhard de Chardin by American Catholics some twenty years after his breakthrough in Europe is symptomatic of a more general problem.

7. See J. M. R. Tillard: *L'Eucharistie, Pâques de l'Eglise,* Paris, 1964.

revitalize our union with Christ in the Holy Spirit. This is the heart of Christian life. For the substance of both our life and our witness is the presence of the Redeemer. The Eucharistic presence is "real," for Christ really transforms bread and wine into his body and blood; and it is also "spiritual," for Christ becomes present to faith. Neither flesh nor blood sees him; only faith knows. The Eucharistic presence is achieved in a prayer of thanksgiving the liturgical structure of which forms a detailed thanksgiving for the great events in which we have shared through Baptism and Confirmation: creation, the incarnation, the resurrection, the ascension. Only because Baptism and Confirmation have made us partakers in the messianic priesthood of Christ can we give thanks. At this time our share in the royal priesthood becomes so actual that Christ the High Priest is himself sacramentally present among us, and our thanksgiving becomes his thanksgiving. In the mystery of the Eucharist we are transformed into the Mystical Body of Christ; we become the outward shape adopted today by the messiahship of the Only Son.

Thus the common priesthood of the People demands a theology of the ministerial priesthood. This function, within the sacramental framework of the People, is destined to preserve the good order of the Christian gathering, mainly, but not only, in the celebration of the meal of Thanksgiving. As the Council maintains, "Although they differ from one another in essence and not only in degree, the common priesthood of the faithful and the ministerial or hierarchical priesthood are nonetheless ordained to each other" (art. 10). The common priesthood of the faithful, given through Baptism and Confirmation, and exercised in all the sacraments (art. 11), ontologically transforms our old being into a new creature. The priesthood of the clergy is a functional empowerment, conferred by Christ, to perform the sacramental re-enactment of the Last Supper, by which our initiation to Christian life reaches its climax, and in which we recognize the presence of the Lord at the breaking of the Bread.

* * *

Some reflections may be made at this point concerning the three qualities of kingship, priesthood and prophethood as applied to the People of God. The Council speaks only of priesthood and prophethood in the context of the chapter on the People, yet this is completed later: kingship, or regimen, or government, is treated at length in the chapter on the hierarchy, and the laity's share in the kingship of Christ is described in Chapter V, article 36, in keeping with a noted address of Bishop De Smedt.[8]

All three functions belong to the People of God as a whole and to each Christian in particular. Chapter V will carefully point this out by explaining how all three functions of God's People are to be manifested in the life of the Christian layman (arts. 34–36). Kingship and priesthood are directly implied in the scriptural doctrine of the "royal priesthood," itself grounded in the Covenant with Moses as formulated, for instance, in Exodus 19:5–6:

If you will obey my voice indeed and keep my Covenant, then you shall be a peculiar treasure unto me above all people; for all the earth is mine; and you shall be unto me a kingdom of priests and a holy nation.

Prophethood is applied to the faithful in the line of the Pauline doctrine on the Church's foundation on the apostles and the

8. In O'Hanlon, *Council Speeches of Vatican II*, pp. 39–43.

prophets. It stresses the fact that the People of God today is the messianic people foretold by the prophet Joel:

I will pour out my Spirit upon all flesh; and your sons and your daughters shall prophesy, your old men shall dream dreams and your young men shall see visions. [Joel 2:28]

In the messianic era, in which the Church lives, all the People of God is *king,* sitting already upon twelve thrones to judge the twelve tribes of Israel; *priest,* who, in the words by which the Roman liturgy describes the liturgical function of the laity, "offers the sacrifice of praise" announced by the prophet Malachi (1:11); *prophet,* crying "Abba, Father," in which utterance "the Spirit of God joins with our spirit in testifying that we are God's children" (Rom 8:16).[9]

One may ask, however, how these biblical and traditional categories of kingship, priesthood and prophecy relate to the concrete functions of the Christian People in our times. The implications of biblical revelation and of theological tradition should be meaningful today, and it is not enough for a Council to borrow biblical categories, if these are to remain a closed book to the technically uninitiated.

Contemporary Catholic theology has attempted to make these categories meaningful. By a frequent mistake, many Protestants seem to think that the doctrine of the priesthood of all believers was rediscovered by Luther after the dark ages of an excessively clerical Catholicism. In a recent volume, *The Priesthood of All Believers,* Cyril Eastwood finds it possible to jump, in his historical survey of the question, from "the writings of the early Fathers" to "the appearance of Martin Luther." He mainly blames St. Cyprian for what he calls "a new note," namely: "The High Priestly race gave place to the High Priestly class, and the

9. See Jean Leclercq: *La Royauté du Christ au Moyen Age,* Paris, 1959.

spiritual sacrifices gave place to a priestly sacrifice offered to God in the Eucharist."[10] As has been shown, among others, by Congar and Dabin in scholarly studies[11] and as has been more popularly explained, for instance, by Pius XII in an allocution of November 2, 1954,[12] and by Bishop De Smedt in a pastoral letter of 1961,[13] the doctrine of the common priesthood has ever been an essential point of Catholic teaching. The prophetic or charismatic function of the People of God has also always been maintained, even though its exercise took many diverse forms and encountered, too, many obstacles at all periods. The kingly function of the People, which implies its participation in government, was in fact much more commonly maintained in the Middle Ages than in modern times, when the concentration of government around the bishops and the Pope has reserved regimen to one order—the hierarchy—within the People of God. It is clearly the intention of the Council to open new avenues to reflection on the participation of all in the three functions of Christ: king, prophet, priest.

On what these may mean in our times I would suggest the following remarks.

For historical reasons, the notion of *kingship* is obviously alien to this country, and is increasingly foreign to most parts of the world. Yet the meaning of kingship is germane to that of dominion, domination; and our entire modern civilization attempts

10. *The Priesthood of All Believers,* Minneapolis, 1962, p. xii. A much better understanding of the position of the problem will be found in Alden D. Kelley (Anglican): *The People of God. A Study in the Doctrine of the Laity,* Greenwich, Conn., 1962.

11. See footnotes 2 and 3.

12. Address *Magnificate Dominum* (*Acta Apostolicae Sedis,* 1954, pp. 666–777).

13. See footnote 3.

to dominate the world by way of technology. To say that the Christian People is "king" amounts to saying that it has been given dominion over all things. "The spiritual man judges all things and he is judged by no one" (1 Cor. 2:15). He has been given Lordship over the universe. The dominion which the Creator entrusted to Adam and which was embodied in the Noachic Covenant belongs to the People of God as the spiritual representative of mankind. In other words, the function of the People of God is to enter the world of dominion and mastery over nature, the world of science, of engineering, of planning and of government, with the interpretation of creation as sacrament of the divine, as channel and instrument of God's communication with man, as vehicle of awesome and numinous power, which is implied in the Christion Gospel. This wide field is, properly speaking, the domain of the layman, who, by his technical knowledge, belongs to this world and, by his commitment to the Gospel, can interpret it in a way which no other technician knows. Into this world the cleric occasionally and exceptionally may enter fruitfully, but the clergy as a whole lacks competence because it usually does not have the required scientific and technical knowledge at its disposal. This is the realm of what Pius XI called "the consecration of the world," an expression used in the transitive form, "to consecrate the world," in article 34 of the constitution: "As worshippers acting in all things in holiness, laymen consecrate the world itself to God."

The notion of *priesthood* is unfortunately no less obscure to our contemporaries, for the reason that it has been onesidedly connected, in the popular mind and in popular theology, with the specific work and calling of priests and ministers. This is not special to Catholics, for whom the Eucharistic priesthood has specific sacramental value; it is also widespread among

Protestant laymen, who find it just as hard, I believe, to relate the notion of universal priesthood to their task as laymen. Yet the modern liturgical movement may enable us to make priesthood relevant again as a function of the whole People. The common priesthood is exercised first of all by taking part in liturgical worship. Liturgical participation means precisely that the liturgy is not performed by the clergy and witnessed by the laity sitting as spectators in the pews; it is celebrated rather by the entire People of God, each member fulfilling his task in the hierarchical order of the Supper. All Christians need to recover and restore the sense of organic action, of corporate prayer, of collective praise, thanksgiving and adoration, which is the heart of worship. In this organic cult only can the People of God find a proper basis for its further priestly function of offering to God, day by day, the spiritual sacrifice of a contrite heart.

The notion of *prophecy* is equally unknown today.[14] Yet the fact that men are looking for leadership and that, recently and at this very time, leaders and false prophets with merely human magnetism have been able to command the allegiance of millions, shows that we can still understand the meaning of spiritual power. There can be no false prophet where there is no longing for a "word from the Lord." And where false prophets appear, there is a possibility for true prophets to arise and, perchance, to be heard. The Christian prophet must bear witness, in our alienated world, to the good news that the apparently absurd conditions of existence—estrangement within and without us, alienation between man and man, misunderstandings and strifes between ideologies, dichotomy between object and subject, cadu-

14. See John Henry Newman: *The Prophetical Office of the Church*, 1837; Yves Congar: *Vraie et Fausse Réforme dans l'Eglise;* Karl Rahner: *The Dynamic Element in the Church*, New York, 1964.

city of friendship and love—do make sense in Jesus Christ, who by his resurrection from the dead has assigned a purpose to all deaths. In him alone all things are recapitulated; they start again from the beginning and they find poise and balance in him. He alone is the Way, the Truth and the Life. The prophetic function of the People of God is simply to bear witness to Christ, to be ready at all times to "give an account of the faith that is in us," to offer oneself to the Holy Spirit as a willing instrument of apostolate and evangelism.

Kingship, priesthood and prophecy may be translated as service, worship and witness. The priesthood of the People of God is a service to the world where we live; a worship of God, Creator and Redeemer; and a witnesst to Christ, the Alpha and the Omega, the First and the Last.

One important topic essentially connected with the theme of the People of God still remains to be examined, namely the difficult question of membership in the People. Who belongs to the People of God? Before we can answer this, we should pay attention to the Council's use of the image "pilgrim People" or "pilgrim Church." The People of God is on a pilgrimage. This comes back time and again in the constitution *De Ecclesia.* "The new Israel . . . in search of a future and abiding city" (art. 9), "moving forward through trials and tribulations" (art. 9): these expressions imply the classical opposition between the status of the believer *in via,* the *viator,* as opposed to the *comprehensor* in heaven. The pilgrim way is the way of faith, in which we march slowly toward the vision that will make us *comprehensores,* when faith will give way to sight and we may see God face to face.

This approach makes it possible to conceive of the Church as made up, at different levels, of all those who are, in one form or another, "on the way," and who share, to some degree at least, the status of faith, perceiving God "as through a glass, darkly" (1 Cor. 13:18). Accordingly, the *De Ecclesia* considers three successive levels of those who belong to the People of God: firstly, "the Catholic faithful" (art. 14); secondly, "all those who, being baptized, bear the name of Christian, yet do not profess the faith in its integrity or do not keep the unity of communion with the successor of Peter" (art. 15); thirdly, "those who have not yet received the Gospel" (art. 16).[15] These three degrees of appurtenance to the People are set between two important paragraphs: the catholicity of the People of God, to which all men are somehow related (art. 13); and the missionary nature and function of the Church, by which the catholicity of God's People grows toward perfection little by little (art. 17).

What is catholicity? The Council formulates the answer in this suggestive sentence:

This mark of universality, which adorns the People of God, is the gift from the Lord himself, by which the Catholic Church is effectively and always oriented toward the recapitulation of all mankind with all its goods, under its Head, Christ, in the unity of His Spirit. [art. 13]

Thus, catholicity is a datum, a gift freely bestowed on the People of God; yet it is also a potentiality, for it opens the Church to all mankind and makes her effectively able to prepare and anticipate the recapitulation of all things in Christ. The word *recapitulation* is clearly to be taken in its patristic sense, as it is used by St. Irenaeus, to whom a footnote refers.[16] Irenaeus's doctrine is

15. See Pope Paul VI's references to the need to perfect the Church's catholicity: sermon for Pentecost 1964; encyclical *Ecclesiam Suam;* and the Pope's speeches on the occasion of his journey to Bombay (in *Documentation Catholique,* n. 1439, January 1965).

16. Chapter II of the constitution, article 10; the reference is to Irenaeus: *Adversus Haereses,* III, 16, 6; III, 22, 1–3.

inspired by the Pauline concepts of Christ as the Head (*caput*) and of the Church as the *pleroma* or fullness of Christ. The internal catholicity of the Church is the unity and unanimity of her members: the individual members "gathered from many peoples" (art. 13) into the People of God, and what the Council calls the "particular Churches enjoying their own tradition without detriment to the primacy of the chair of Peter which presides over the universal assembly of love" (art. 13). This aspect of diversity in unity is suitably emphasized, thus preserving the organic nature of the Body, which is one in its diversity and diverse in its unity.[17]

There is also an external catholicity, or rather a catholicity turned outside, open upon the world around, which is never closed but always prepared to welcome new members in the Body of Christ and new aspects of creation to the fullness of the *pleroma,* so that God may be all in all in his People. This is the meaning of this sentence: "All men are called to belong to this Catholic unity of the People of God, which heralds and promotes universal peace" (art. 13).[18]

On the one hand, all men are called and they are thus, even unknowingly, turned to the People of God. Catholics, other Christians, the People of the Jews, "in its election, most dear on account of the patriarchs" (art. 16), the "sons of Ishmael, who, acknowledging Abraham as their Father, believe also in the God of Abraham" (art. 16), all those also who, "with no fault of their own have not yet reached an express acknowledgement of God":

17. On the Church's internal unity, see two addresses by Paul VI, on January 22, 1964 (*Documentation Catholique,* n. 1418, cols. 233–234), and on March 31, 1965 (*l. c.,* n. 1446, cols. 675–678).

18. Concerning external catholicity, one should compare the constitution *De Ecclesia* with the Council's Decree on Ecumenism and its Declaration on Non-Christian Religions.

all are turned toward the Church, if not in faith, at least in the hope which is implicit in their nearness to God, who, in the words of the Council, "is not far from them, for he gives life, inspiration and all things to all men, and the Saviour wants all men to be saved" (art. 16). Thus all men in some way belong to the Church, being essentially oriented toward communion with the People of God.

On the other hand, the Church is also existentially turned toward all men. This is her mission, —defined by Christ in terms of "teaching all nations," —transmitted by the Apostles in terms of "announcing the saving truth," —acknowledged with fear and trembling by St. Paul: "Woe to me if I do not evangelize!" (1 Cor. 9:16), —kept alive by the Holy Spirit. This implies "preaching the Gospel," "cleansing, raising up and perfecting for the glory of God whatever good is found planted in the hearts and the minds of men, and in their rites and cultures" (art. 17). It implies also baptizing, and above all "bringing to completion the upbuilding of the Body of Christ in the Eucharistic sacrifice," so that the prophecy may be fulfilled: "From the rising to the setting of the sun, my name is great among the nations, and in every place a pure oblation is sacrificed and offered to my Name" (Mal. 1:11).

The treatment of the theme of the People of God by the Council ends on this missionary note. The mission is not only presented as an imperative of the Church's life and as constitutive of her structure; it is also seen as an anticipation of the eschatological return of all things to the Father. We may quote to this effect the last sentence of Chapter II:

Thus the Church together prays and toils, that the fulness of the whole world may pass into the People of God, the Body of the Lord and the Temple of the Holy Spirit, and that in Christ, the Head of all,

all honor and glory may be rendered to the Creator and Father of all. [art. 17]

Concluding our survey of the Council's doctrine on the People of God, we may say that two major points stand out.

In the first place, the Council has not "changed" any specific Catholic teaching. On the contrary, a line of continuity clearly goes from the ecclesiology developed in theological circles in the last few decades to the thought of the last Popes, especially Pius XII, and the constitution *Lumen Gentium*.

In the second place, the difficult point of Catholic ecclesiology—that is, the unity of the invisible, mysteric aspect of the Church with her visible, institutional status—is thrown into light and is made, I believe, less vulnerable to criticism by the mediation of the biblical and traditional concept of the People of God. The two, though never to be separated, aspects of the Church, by which she is a spiritual, God-given reality in an earthly, human organization, are joined at the middle level of the Church as the People gathered from Jews and Gentiles and carrying the Good News to all nations, which she initiates into the realm of salvation. As a People, the Church is of the earth, earthly; as the People of God, she is of heaven, heavenly. In her those who were "Not-My-People" are now addressed by God as "My-People." The institutional elements which have provided the Church with her historical shape cannot be opposed to the spiritual Event of God's descent. Rather, by embodying her stability and continuity and by expressing the unanimity of the People, they also convey the mystery hidden in God, finally revealed to his People and through it to the world.

IV.

The Hierarchy

As IT WAS presented to the Council and debated in its second
and third sessions, the question of the Church's hierarchy drew
much more attention than any other aspect of ecclesiology.
There are good reasons for this. Firstly, many of the disagree-
ments between Rome and Orthodoxy and between Rome and
Protestantism hinge on the answer to that question. Secondly, the
Catholic Church apparently runs counter on this point to the so
called democratic trends of our times, for she maintains a
"medieval" structure, when all "modern" nations have adopted
systems of government derived from the philosophy of the Enlightenment and its political sequels in the American and the
French Revolutions, and when the erstwhile autocratic structures
of many Protestant establishments have followed the secular
trend toward giving more voice, at least on paper and nomi-
nally, to the common man. Thirdly, the contemporary Church
situation has inherited a handicap from the last century, when
the Ist Vatican Council, attempting to stem the tide of secularism
and its undermining of many sections of Christendom, solemnly

defined the infallibility of the Bishop of Rome when he formulates *"ex cathedra* definitions."

Indeed, it was the general opinion, soon after the announcement of the future Council by Pope John XXIII, that the major task to be done concerned doctrinal adjustment by which the doctrine of Vatican I on papal infallibility would be completed and perhaps counterbalanced by a doctrinal exposé on other aspects of Church government, and especially on the diffuse authority of the bishops at large and on their concentrated authority in Council.[1] One opportunely remembered that the work of the Ist Vatican Council had been left unfinished by the start of the Franco-Prussian War of 1870. The bishops, who had been meeting since the 8th of December 1869, went home after the fourth session of the Council, which ended on the 18th of July 1870, and most of the agenda was left practically untouched. In particular, the dogmatic constitution *De Ecclesia Christi,* which treated at length of the powers of the Supreme Pontiff, did not speak, except by implication, of the powers of the bishops in general. As a result, the world, which did not study the inner workings of the Council, was given the impression, admittedly shared by many a Catholic, that from now on, the Pope's authority alone mattered, the bishops being reduced to the status of executive officers of papal decisions.

In approaching the study of the IInd Vatican Council, one should take account also of Orthodox reactions to the definition of papal infallibility,[2] and of the increasing importance, within the Catholic Church, of the theology and traditions of the

1. Hans Küng: *The Council, Reform and Reunion,* New York, 1961.
2. See "Primacy and Primacies in the Orthodox Church" (*St. Vladimir's Seminary Bulletin,* vol. 4, 1960, nn. 2–3).

Oriental Churches in communion with Rome. It is a matter of history that the definition of papal infallibility provoked a schism which, relatively minor though it was, was nonetheless a scandal. Although the Old Catholic Church, in spite of early efforts, could not reach such an agreement with the Orthodox Churches that they might form one communion, it did express some of the reactions to papal infallibility that the Orthodox world also felt. The definition represented, in the mind of the Old Catholic Church, a temporary development, due to the excessive reaction of the Counter-Reformation against Protestantism, of the age-old belief in the primacy of Peter; but, as it was a predominantly Latin development, it did not couch its doctrine in terms that all could recognize as expressing the entire tradition of the Catholic Church of East and West, of past and present. While the Old Catholics rejected papal infallibility in the name of St. Cyprian, of late medieval conciliarism and the Council of Basle, of more recent Gallicanism and Josephism and the Synod of Pistoia, the Orthodox Churches, firm in their belief in the primacy of Peter and in a historical primacy of honor recognized by the Fathers to the Bishop of Rome, could not reconcile the Latin categories of the Ist Vatican Council with the tradition of the Eastern Fathers and of the eight Ecumenical Councils known to them. For even though the Council of Chalcedon had acclaimed Pope Leo's doctrinal authority, its 28th canon had also attributed the origin of the primacy to political and cultural reasons. That the validity of this canon had never been acknowledged in Rome did not affect its impact on Orthodox ecclesiology.

The theological atmosphere in Roman Catholicism since the Second World War had been marked by a return to both biblical and patristic sources. Here, as in the liturgical movement which gained strength at the same time, Orthodoxy acquired a value that older generations of Roman Catholics had all but forgotten: it was seen as the faithful image of the Church of the Fathers and of the great Councils. While Western theology was reading Origen and the Cappadocians, St. John Chrysostom and St. John Damascene, it could not ignore the ecclesiology which had grown out of the Eastern patristic tradition, and which was faithfully preserved in the Orthodox communion. The desire to express the Catholic concept of the Church in better than merely Latin terms and in a wider and older doctrinal context than the theology of the Counter-Reformation came to appear to many as one of the major challenges facing the Church today. In these conditions, the Council called by John XXIII appeared as a providential occasion to restore to Catholic theology some of the dimensions that the times of estrangement from Byzantium and of increasing concentration on the Catholic-Protestant separations had obscured, and which had been all but lost to the Catholic consciousness.

Precisely at that time, the Melkite Church, that is, a section of the old Patriarchate of Antioch in communion with Rome since 1701, formulated, through the voice of its Patriarch, His Beatitude Maximos IV, and several of its bishops, a theological position through which an authentic echo of Orthodoxy was heard within the confines of the Catholic Communion.[3] It called for an enlarging of the catholicity of the Church by making it less Western and Latin and by opening it, not only to the traditional cultures of the East, but also, as a consequence, to the new Christian cultures which should soon appear in the missionary enclaves of the

3. Maximos IV Sayegh (ed.): *The Eastern Churches and Catholic Unity*, New York, 1963.

Asian and the African world. How to express this in our theology of the Church, how to broaden our concept of the Institution to allow for the maximum freedom possible for the development of native Catholicisms in the larger part of the world—which is non-European and therefore untouched, in principle at least, by the juridical categories of Latin theology and of Roman Canon Law—was bound to loom large in the concerns of the bishops and the "experts" who found their way to Rome for the sessions of the IInd Vatican Council.[4]

* * *

The conciliar treatment of the topic "hierarchy" follows the classical pattern of Catholic thought: Jesus Christ selected the apostles, to whom he entrusted the task of preaching the Gospel to all nations; the bishops succeeded the apostles, not of course in their quality as eyewitnesses of the deeds of the Lord Incarnate, but in their functions as preachers of the Gospel; the Lord selected Peter to lead the apostles, and the bishops of Rome succeeded Peter in the primacy; as a consequence of their mission of preaching, the bishops also share the powers of Christ as Teacher, Priest and King, in their own function of teaching, sanctifying and governing the Church; finally, priests and deacons are associated to the bishops for the fulfillment of their duties. All this is conventional enough. To a great extent, it simply restates what was already said by Vatican I in its constitution *Pastor Aeternus*,[5]

4. See O'Hanlon, *Council Speeches of Vatican II*, pp. 231–288; Edward Schillebeeckx: "The Church and Mankind" (*Concilium: The Church and Mankind*, Glen Rock, 1965, pp. 68–101).

5. Text in *Conciliorum Oecumenicorum Decreta*, Herder, Freiburg 1962, pp. 787–792, or D.S., 3050–3075 (ET: in John H. Leith (ed.): *Creeds of the Churches*, New York, 1963, pp. 448–457).

with the difference that the exposé of *Pastor Aeternus* was focussed all but exclusively on Peter and the Bishop of Rome, while
that of *Lumen Gentium* is broader and includes all the apostles
and all the bishops.

Yet some elements are sufficiently new to mark a significant
change of perspective.

The sacramentality of the episcopal consecration is clearly
affirmed (art. 21):

> This Holy Synod teaches that by episcopal consecration the fullness
> of the sacrament of Orders is conferred, which is called the high priest-
> hood and the summit of the sacred ministry in the liturgical practice
> of the Church and by the Holy Fathers.

It is further said in the same paragraph:

> It is clear from the tradition expressed especially in the liturgical rites
> of the East and the West that by the imposition of hands and the words
> of consecration the grace of the Holy Spirit is conferred and a sacred
> character is imprinted, so that the bishops share eminently and visibly
> in the functions of Christ as Teacher, Pastor and Pontiff.

The intention of this text is not to decide the historical question of the origin of episcopacy: Did it start as a monarchic
episcopate, as it is now? Or rather as a pluralistic presbytery, out
of which a leading presbyter emerged, to whom the formerly
generic title of bishop came to be reserved? Historical scholarship
can still debate this question, which concerns facts of the history
of apostolic and post-apostolic times, but need not affect the
present structure of the Church's hierarchy.[6] Nor is it the Council's intention to solve the problem of the few cases in which
priests, who were not in bishops' orders, may in the past have

6. On the origin of episcopacy, see Jean Colson: *L'Evêque dans les Com-
munautés Primitives,* Paris, 1951.

consecrated other priests to the priesthood or even to the episcopate.[7] The purpose of this declaration is to remove the episcopal
function from the increasingly administrative realm in which the
growth of ecclesiastical bureaucracy has tended to confine it, on
the pattern of the bureaucratic government of modern societies.
The bishop is essentially a "hierarch," a sacred person fulfilling
a sacred function. The trend that transforms bishops into businessmen—occupied with buying land, building churches, schools
and hospitals, supervising parishes and assigning priests to their
functions in the most efficient way possible—runs counter to the
Catholic concept of the sacred, which is centered on the liturgical
function of the bishops. In the liturgy over which he presides and
which is offered by and for his entire diocese, the bishop is the
high priest expressing the unity of the Church as a communion,
in whom the People of God gathered together for worship finds
a voice formulating its common prayer. One cannot therefore
interpret this emphasis on the sacramentality of episcopal consecration as ending the debate between those who consider the
bishop as a priest, whose responsibility for the whole Church of
Christ in a certain locality gives him a unique function in the
Eucharistic priesthood, and those who believe that the bishop has
qualitatively and quantitatively more priesthood than the priest.[8]
In any case, the bishop enjoys the fullness of the priesthood, although the Council does not decide if he alone has been granted
the fullness of its *essence,* or if what the episcopal consecration
gives him is the fullness of its *exercise.* The relevance of this
declaration lies in the sacramental orientation that it gives to the

7. See the bull *Sacrae Religionis* of Boniface IX (1400) and the with-
drawal in 1403 of the privileges it conceded: D.S., 1145–1146.
8. See St. Thomas, *Summa Theologica, suppl.,* q. 40, a. 5.

episcopate. In the long run, it should help to develop a generation of preaching and liturgical bishops rather than one of building and administering bishops. Thus the hierarchy itself would connote pastoral care rather than ruling.

* * *

A second feature of the constitution has attracted more attention than the sacramentality of the episcopate. Yet the collegiality of the Church, as manifested in and implemented by the episcopal college, directly implies less than the sacramentality of the episcopate already suggests. Sacramentality entails the reawakening of the episcopate to its sacramental meaning and function, whereas collegiality could be accepted and exercised by an unregenerated body of bishops conceiving of their function in terms of power only.

Nothing is fundamentally new in the notion of collegiality as applied to the apostles and to the bishops. In a volume published in 1962, Jérôme Hamer studied the notion of the Church as a communion, a notion which is connected with that of the Mystical Body as explained in the encyclical of Pius XII *Mystici Corporis,* which is intrinsic to the New Testament developments on the Church as the Body and even to the meaning of the term *ecclesia,* or gathering.[9] Finding that Bellarmine's definition of the Church from its purely visible and external aspects is inadequate, and that the sacramental concept of the Church (the Church as sacrament of the Kingdom of God) as explained, among others, by Otto Semmelroth[10] and Karl Rahner,[11] is also insufficient,

9. Jérôme Hamer: *The Church is a Communion.*
10. *Die Kirche als Ursakrament,* Frankfurt, 1953.
11. *Theological Investigations,* vol. 2, Baltimore, 1963.

Hamer proposes a definition that hinges around the notion of *koinonia:* "The Church is the Mystical Body of Christ, that is, an interior and exterior communion, the life of union with Christ signified and caused by the organism of the mediation of Christ."[12] *Koinonia*, communion, is by no means a new concept. It is biblical, for the Church of the New Testament is a communion in Christ and in the Spirit. Hamer shows also that, for the Church Fathers and the Schoolmen, Church communion does not simply connote, as we might think, unity in faith; it also refers to unity of government and organization. Communion is both visible and invisible. It connects all the members of the Body together and to Christ, the Head. Communion is a relational concept denoting relationships at the level of existence (co-existence as interdependence) and of behavior (communion in the same sacraments and the same gracious presence of God in Christ). It is, at the same time, the communion of the saints, saints meaning both sacred things and sacred persons, and the communion of bishop with bishop and of the faithful with their bishop.

The communion of bishop with bishop is essentially identical with their consensus in the transmission of the doctrine "once communicated to the saints," and it is externalized in their consultations, their exchanges of advice, their common attempts to solve common problems and to adopt common attitudes, their pooling of resources at the provincial, national or regional level: this is no other than the collegiality of which Vatican II speaks and which it describes in these terms: "The old practice whereby bishops established in the whole world communicated with each other and with the Roman Bishop in the bonds of unity, love

12. Jérôme Hamer, *L'Eglise est une Communion,* p. 97.

and peace, and the Councils gathered into one to decide difficult problems in common after reflecting on the opinions of the many, show the collegial nature and structure of the episcopal order" (art. 22). Collegiality is the communion of all the bishops together, whether they are gathered in Council or they communicate with each other across the distances that separate them geographically. It may be seen at two levels: that of the essence of episcopacy and that of its exercise. In its essence, the episcopate is one, so that the episcopal college has succeeded the apostolic college as a whole, whereas a bishop is seldom the successor of a given apostle. In its exercise, collegiality requires that the bishops make an effort to keep up and intensify the bonds of unity, love and peace which unite the local Churches into the oneness of the body of Christ. In its essence, collegiality is not reserved to bishops, for the whole body of Christ is collegially one. No liturgical worship is thinkable without the collegial unanimity of all the participants, clergy and laity. No parish fulfills its function properly without a collegial unanimity of the clergy and the laity in the fraternal communion of the People of God.

Catholicity was described, in the preceding chapter of the constitution, as achieved by the Spirit: "For this God sent the Spirit of his Son, who is Lord and life-giver, who, for the whole Church and for each and every faithful, is the principle of their gathering and of their unity in the doctrine and communion of the apostles, in the breaking of the Bread and in prayers" (art. 13). One may conclude, comparing the two chapters, that collegiality is but one aspect of Catholicity, namely that by which the potential universality of the Church, gathering the whole world into one, is anticipated in the cohesiveness of all the members of the Body.

This stress is far from new in recent Councils. Several studies published since the beginning of the preparation of the IInd Vatican Council have shown that collegiality was not absent from the concerns of the bishops at the Ist Vatican Council. That the Fathers of Vatican I were like docile sheep prepared to uphold papal infallibility at the cost of episcopal authority could not be further from the truth. The bishops who were in Rome in 1869–70 were intent on defending and asserting their episcopal rights, and the vindication of the rights and duties of bishops was one of the frequent topics discussed on the floor of the Council. Insistence on this point inspired the following passage of the constitution *Pastor Aeternus:*

So far is this power of the Supreme Pontiff from bearing prejudice to the ordinary and immediate power of episcopal jurisdiction, by which bishops, who have been set by the Holy Spirit to succeed and hold the place of the apostles, to feed and to govern each his own flock as true pastors, that their episcopal authority is really asserted, strengthened and protected by the supreme and universal Pastor, in keeping with the words of St. Gregory the Great: My honor is the honor of the whole Church. My honor is the firm strength of my brethren. I am truly honored, when due honor is not withheld from each and all. [D.S., 3061]

Thus one of the aims and purposes of papal authority, according to Vatican I, is the protection and promotion of episcopal authority.

Furthermore, the authority assigned to the Bishop of Rome in the constitution *Pastor Aeternus* was conceived by the Vatican Fathers on the pattern of episcopal authority. This has been shown especially in Jean-Pierre Torrell's study of the theology of the episcopate at Vatican I.[13] Admittedly, the preceding quota-

13. *La Théologie de l'Episcopat au Premier Concile du Vatican,* Paris, 1961; see also Georges Dejaifve: *Pape et Evêques au Premier Concile du Vatican,* Bruges, 1961; Gustave Thils: *Primauté Pontificale et Prérogatives Episcopales,* Louvain, 1961; Karl Rahner and Joseph Ratzinger: *The Episcopate*

tion mentions only the local authority of bishops wielding episcopal power each in his own see, and prescinds from the question
of their share of universal authority over all the Church. However, the constitution *Pastor Aeternus* was originally a part—
Chapter XI—of a longer project, *De Ecclesia,* prepared by the
"Deputation of the Faith" and on which the German theologian
Joseph Kleutgen (1811–1883) had the greatest influence. This
draft did acknowledge the bishops' participation in the government of the universal Church. In the name of the "Deputation of
the Faith," Zinelli declared to the Council: "We willingly agree
that full and total ecclesiastical sovereignty over all the faithful
resides also in ourselves as gathered in ecumenical Council, in
ourselves, the bishops united to their head. Yes, this perfectly
fits the Church united to the head. Gathered with their leader in
ecumenical Council, in which case they represent the whole
Church, or dispersed, yet in union with their leader, in which case
they are the Church herself, the bishops therefore have supreme
authority."[14] Thus the "Deputation of the Faith" admitted that
all bishops share supreme authority over the universal Church,
whether they are in Council or in their respective sees. Torrell
concludes: "Although the word is not pronounced, it seems clear
that these perspectives exactly anticipate what is now called episcopal collegiality."[15]

That collegiality is not new may also be gathered from St.
Thomas Aquinas: "The unity of the Church may be seen in two

---

and the Primacy, New York, 1962; Yves Congar and Bernard Dupuy
(eds.): *L'Episcopat et l'Eglise Universelle,* Paris, 1962; James T. Kava-
naugh: "Toward a Theology of the Episcopacy" (*Frontline,* vol. 3, 1965,
pp. 98–126); Journet: *The Church of the Word Incarnate.*

14. Torrell, *op. cit.,* p. 151.
15. *Ibid.,* p. 276.

ways: first, in the connection of the members of the Church
together, or their communication; second, in the orientation of
all the members of the Church toward one head."[16] Under its
first aspect, unity is collegiality; under the second, it is communion witth Christ through the person of the Bishop of Rome.
These two aspects of unity are called by Yves Congar *communion between* and *communion with*.[17] Communion *with,* obedience, has been more emphasized in modern times; yet communion *between*, or mutual fraternal assistance and participation
in each other's responsibility, has always been present in the
Church and was implied even in Counter-Reformation ecclesiology.

There is therefore nothing new in the IInd Vatican Council's
statements on collegiality—except, to some extent, the word. This
section of the conciliar document simply brings into the open
what was understood at the Ist Vatican Council, and incorporates
into the official texts what had been said, and admitted by all,
during the debates in 1870. The collegiality endorsed by Vatican
II is therefore not meant to correct the doctrine of Vatican I, but
to eschew the exaggerations that had misinterpreted Vatican I.
As Patriarch Maximos IV declared during the debates, "the
Council should not be satisfied to repeat what the First Vatican
Council had to say on this point, since there is already an accepted part of the Church's patrimony. What this Council should
do is clarify and complete the words of Vatican I in the light of
the teaching about the divine institution and the inalienable
rights of the episcopate."[18]

16. *Summa Theologica,* II II, q. 39, a. 1.
17. *Jalons pour une Théologie du Laïcat,* p. 465.
18. In O'Hanlon, *Council Speeches of Vatican II,* pp. 72–73.

Since the task was one of completion and clarification of the Catholic doctrine on the episcopal government of the Church, what ought to strike us when we read the somewhat long and involved passages of the constitution *De Ecclesia* about collegiality is not their newness or their boldness, but their shyness. Since by a common accord scholars agree that collegiality is a relatively new word expressing an old reality of Church life and a fundamental quality of the Church's nature as a community, why did the Doctrinal Commission of the Council, which was responsible for preparing this text, and why did the Council as a whole deem it necessary to surround the explanation of collegiality with such caution, and with so many reminders of papal authority? Let us read, for instance, one of the passages where collegiality and papal authority are carefully balanced: "The college or body of bishops has no authority unless it is taken together with the Roman Pontiff, successor of Peter, as its head, the latter's power of primacy over all pastors and faithful being integrally maintained." Or, in another text, "This collegial authority may be exercised by the bishops, together with the Pope, when they are dispersed over the earth, provided that the head of the college calls them to collegial action, or that at least he approves or accepts freely the united action of the dispersed bishops, so that this may be a true collegial act" (art. 22). The college, by definition, includes the Pope as the visible head or primate; yet in both cases the conciliar text redundantly affirms the Pope's independent right of action, so that the Pope appears to be both part of the episcopal college and above it.

That the Pope is both in communion with the other bishops and above them expresses the Catholic concept of one authority in two jurisdictions, one episcopal authority equally residing in the episcopal college, which includes the Pope, and in the Pope as successor of Peter in his primacy over the universal Church. That this had to be repeated over and over again is, however, another matter, which would be disconcerting if we did not keep the perspective of Vatican II in mind.

The original intention of the Council, which was faithfully maintained throughout its proceedings, was not to formulate doctrine in any strikingly new way or to end free discussions among Catholics. It was pastoral. The pastoral aspect of collegiality does not concern its formulation as a doctrine or its acceptance as a principle. At this level there is no difficulty among bishops or theologians. Rather, it resides in finding a practical way of implementing collegiality at the level of the daily government of the Church by her bishops. As Patriarch Maximos IV Sayegh declared during the second session,

We are convinced that what is an obstacle to unity is not the teaching itself on the primacy, which has adequate support in Holy Scripture and the tradition of the Church, but exaggerated interpretations, and even more, the concrete exercise of the primacy, where, to authentically divine elements and a legitimate ecclesial development, unfortunate borrowings have been more or less consciously added which are patterned on the forms of exercise of purely human authority.[19]

The difficulty is to embody collegiality in an institution which will somehow represent the bishops and act in their name in conjunction with the Bishop of Rome as primate. The texts of the Council are simply preparatory of such an institution. They have a propedeutic or prospective purpose, the full meaning of which will come to light when the "Episcopal Synod," created by Paul VI

19. *Ibid.,* p. 72.

to implement collegiality, has been in successful operation for some time.

Thus the conciliar treatment of collegiality is still incomplete and, like the preceding work of Vatican II concerning papal authority, it calls for a clarification that must come in due time and that it would be inopportune to anticipate. Yet the broad area of this clarification may be indicated.

The approach of Vatican I to problems of authority was jurisdictional. That of Vatican II has been pastoral, although it has not been able to prescind from problems of jurisdiction and it has paid a tribute to the legalistic mind of Latin theology. The unfinished task is that of exorcising juridicism out of ecclesiology. The passage of the *De Ecclesia* on collegiality represents a courageous attempt to join a theological view of the Church to a juridical view. The task of freeing ecclesiology from the shackles of legalism is, however, not over yet. From this point of view, the ecclesiological doctrine of Vatican II is transitional. It calls for a complement, the principle of which is already established in the views of the Church as Mystery and as People of God. That the Mystery expresses itself in "mystical" actions and "mystical" institutions should be understood from the standpoint of the mystery itself. That the People of God should be given a structure with visible social aspects can also be understood from the point of view of the People. The junction of an ecclesiology of the Mystery and an ecclesiology of the People demands an ecclesiology of unanimity and of the spiritual woof and warp without which unanimity cannot be reached among millions intellectually and emotionally formed by a wide variety of human cultures. Ultimately, the collegiality of government will have to be set in the wider context of the mystery of a People called to represent all mankind before God: what structures and what internal relationships will evolve from the universal vocation of the People of God still remains a secret hidden in God and which the Spirit will unfold in his own good time. The IInd Vatican Council's treatment of collegiality constitutes a milestone in this development.

* * *

One point in the Council's explanations of episcopal collegiality deserves special attention.

For the question comes to mind: What can the meaning of papal infallibility be in relation to the opening of the Church's structure to the requirements of a missionary and eschatologically oriented catholicity? The Ist Vatican Council defined papal infallibility in these terms:

> We teach and define as a divinely revealed dogma that the Roman Pontiff—when he speaks *ex cathedra,* that is, when, in discharge of the office of pastor and doctor of all Christians, by virtue of his supreme apostolic authority, he defines a doctrine of faith or morals to be held by the Universal Church—enjoys, through the divine assistance promised him in St. Peter, the infallibilty with which the divine Redeemer willed his Church to be endowed in defining doctrines of faith or morals; and therefore that these definitions of the Roman Pontiff are, by themselves, and not by consent of the Church, irreformable.[20]

This definition has been a stumbling block in theological conversations between Catholics and Protestants, as well as Catholics and Orthodox. In the main, two objections have been leveled at it. The first is typically Protestant: the definition assumes that the Church is infallible. I will not deal with this objection, for the corresponding statement of Vatican II brings no new argu-

20. D.S., 3073–3074.

ment to it: the infallibility of the Church in union with Christ and under the guidance of the Spirit is and has always been a cornerstone of the Catholic tradition.

The second objection is more subtle and has, it would seem, more validity: it bears on the assertion that papal definitions are irreformable by themselves and not by the consent of the Church. Serious studies of the Ist Vatican Council, however, have pointed out that this definition was not intended to isolate the Pope from the Church or, still less, to give the Pope the right to impose his own beliefs upon a reluctant Church that would not recognize its faith in what he is defining. One of the reporters on the text on infallibility explained at length in the Council that the fact that "the consent of the Church" does not condition papal infallibility cannot mean that it may be missing when the Roman Pontiff has solemnly defined a doctrine. As he said with suitable clarity, "We cannot separate the Pope from the consent of the Church, for this consent could never be wanting. Since we believe that the Pope is infallible as a result of a divine assistance, we thereby believe that the Church's consent can never fail him, since it is impossible for the body of the bishops to be severed from its head and since the Universal Church cannot fall."[21] In other words, the Council refused to make consent a legal restriction on the Pope, and inserted this into its definition of infallibility; but it never thought that the Pope could define one thing, and the consensus of the Church believe another. In view of the debates before the adoption of the definition, its misunderstanding among Protestant authors seems to me unbelievable: infallibility has been taken to imply the replacement of the Church's Tradition by the papal will to power, the total subservience of

21. Torrell, *op. cit.*, p. 187.

the whole Church to the arbitrary decisions of one man, and the end to the practice of holding Ecumenical Councils.[22]

However this may be, the IInd Vatican Council has done its best to clear up this matter and to render further misunderstandings of papal infallibility along these lines unthinkable. The relevant passage runs as follows:

The infallibility with which the divine Redeemer willed his Church to be endowed in defining doctrine of faith or morals extends as far as the deposit of divine revelation, which must be religiously guarded and faithfully expounded. By his function, the Roman Pontiff, head of the college of bishops, enjoys infallibility when, as supreme pastor of all the faithful, who confirms his brothers in the faith, he proclaims a doctrine of faith or morals by definitive action. Therefore his definitions are rightly said to be irreformable of themselves, and not by the consent of the Church, for they are pronounced under the assistance of the Holy Spirit which was promised him in Blessed Peter, and therefore they need no approval by others and they allow of no appeal to another sentence. For then the Roman Pontiff does not pass judgment as a private person, but explains or protects the doctrine of the Catholic faith as the supreme doctor of the Universal Church, in whom the charism of infallibility of this Church resides personally. The infallibility promised to the Church resides also in the body of the bishops, when it exercises the supreme magisterium with the successor of Peter. To these definitions the assent of the Church can never fail to be given, owing to the action of the same Holy Spirit, by whom the flock of Christ is kept and grows in the unity of the faith. [art. 25]

The process we have already observed may be seen again here: the IInd Vatican Council has incorporated into its pronouncement an intention expressed in the debates of Vatican I, yet not included in the constitution *Pastor Aeternus*. This provides us with an authentic interpretation of papal infallibility. The

22. An instance of this misinterpretation will be found in Geddes Mac-Gregor: *The Vatican Revolution*, Boston, 1957; for the interpretation of Vatican I by the Catholic bishops, see the "Declaration of the German Bishops" of 1875, reprinted in Hans Küng, *op. cit.*, pp. 193–201.

Church's consent is not prerequisite to a definition, yet the Church's assent cannot be missing, for the Holy Spirit is committed both to the papal definition and to the Church's assent, which expresses her faith. By the same token, this interpretation of papal infallibility disproves the belief, which still lingers in some non-Catholic circles, that modern Catholicism, especially since 1870, has replaced the primacy of Tradition by the primacy of the Pope. The Church's assent expresses her Tradition. What it assents to is essentially the traditional interpretation of Scripture in the Church, which itself provides the ground for the exercise of papal infallibility. What the Pope, or, for that matter, the Council, defines, is the object of the Church's assent, and, as such, cannot be separated from this assent. It cannot be other than what the Church already assents to, since it must be included, according to the above quotation, in the revelation. And as revelation reaches post-apostolic times through the Church's meditation of the Scriptures as fulfilled in the sacramental events of her spiritual life and as mirrored in the intellectual contemplation of her doctors, papal and conciliar infallibility does nothing more than formulate what the "sense of the Church" perceives less distinctly.

In the context of our document, and even apart from the Council's constitution *De Revelatione,* we may therefore conclude that papal infallibility not only respects the value of the still undefined Catholic Tradition, but is also compatible with a certain "primacy of Scripture," understood of course in a non-exclusive sense. This may be gathered from the following sentence:

When the Roman Pontiff or the body of the bishops together with him define a doctrine, they pronounce it in keeping with revelation itself, which all are bound to stand by and conform to, which is integrally transmitted in Scripture or Tradition through the legitimate succession of the bishops and first of all as the Roman Pontiff's concern, and which, under the light of the Holy Spirit, is religiously kept and faithfully expounded in the Church. [art. n. 25]

* * *

The amount of space I have devoted to infallibility should not overshadow one of the major contributions of the constitution *De Ecclesia* to a theology of the hierarchy. To the popular mind of those who have no hierarchy, the word itself invokes power and implies that the relations between bishops and laymen are those of command and obedience. To those, however, who live in or under a hierarchical system of Church government, hierarchy evokes first of all the sense of the numinous. The bishop remains today, so many centuries after Denys the Areopagite, a hierarch, one who holds sacred functions and who is distinguished from others precisely by the awesomeness of his unity with the celestial Hierarch, Jesus Christ. The hierarchy on earth images the hierarchy in heaven. Accordingly, if a bishop is a ruler, this is not in a political sense; and he should approach his ruling function as a father and a pastor rather than as a superior. And the bishop is not only a ruler, but also, as a hierarch must be when he transmits to lower hierarchical degrees what he has received from higher degrees, a sanctifier and a teacher.

These three aspects of the bishop's function are given due importance in the constitution (art. 25: teaching; art. 26: sanctification; art. 27: government). The task of sanctification deserves special attention, for it highlights one of the major problems met by bishops everywhere. The archbishop of Durban (South Africa), Denis Hurley, noted during the debates that a bishop today cannot fulfill his functions of teaching, sanctifying and ruling directly: he needs to rely on priests as "his hands and feet, his eyes and ears ... indeed, even his voice." "We all know," the archbishop said with a sense of humor, "how much it depends on the way a priest reads out his pastoral letters whether the bishops' words will resound like an archangel's trumpet or drone on like the columns of a telephone directory."[23] This illustrates the fact that it has become more and more difficult for bishops to function as pastors. They may rule from the distance of their palace or the remoteness of their chancery office; but they can hardly be pastors and fathers to their people. There are not enough direct contacts between the supreme pastor of a diocese and the people. Practically everything reaches the bishop through the mediation of any number of ecclesiastical middlemen, priests in parishes or bureaucrats in diocesan offices. When we come to the Supreme Pastor in the Church, this problem is infinitely compounded by the extent of his responsibilities and by the number of officials in his Curia.

The purpose of the IInd Vatican Council being primarily pastoral, its concern has been to help the bishops to be pastors again. This should appear from other documents, especially from the decree on the "pastoral care of dioceses" and the one on the priesthood, the first version of which was rejected by the Council's third session because it was insufficiently pastoral. This also transpires in the constitution *Lumen Gentium*. Thus the bishops are reminded that their task is to celebrate the Holy Eucharist, to "offer the worship of Christian religion to the divine Majesty," to "pray and labor" for the People, "through the ministry of the word to communicate God's power to those who believe unto salvation" (art. 26). They are to use, not only "authority and sacred power," but also "counsel, exhortations, example" for the "edification of their flock in truth and holiness"; "a bishop, sent

23. In O'Hanlon, *Council Speeches of Vatican II*, pp. 108–109.

by the Father to govern his family, must keep before his eyes the example of the Good Shepherd, who came not to be ministered unto, but to minister and to lay down his life for his sheep" (art. 27).

Our last concern is also our first: Catholic bishops, as we said at the beginning of this chapter, need to recover the numinous aspect of their functions, and to convert themselves from ecclesiastical businessmen into pastors and fathers of their flocks. This is not merely a practical problem. It is fundamentally a theological one. For the Catholic hierarchy claims to belong to the essential structure of the People of God. Therefore it has to be from, for and in the People, "taken from among men and beset with weakness," able thereby to "be compassionate for those who lie in ignorance and error" (art. 27). The ultimate theological issue is courageously faced by the Council at this point: Shall the development of the hierarchy, in its self-conception and in its style of life, justify it as the structure of the People of God? Is it the structure that the People of God gives itself in a self-renewing and life-giving Tradition, or is it a yoke imposed on the People by a petrified ecclesiasticism?[24]

The answer of the Catholic faith is that the hierarchy belongs to and in the People of God, from which it is inseparable. But it is an unending task of the Church's on-going reform to render its structures more translucent to the Spirit.

24. This estimate of the Council's achievement obviously disagrees with most journalistic accounts of the question, for example Xavier Rynne: *Letters from Vatican City* (New York, 1963 and 1966); Robert Kaiser: *Pope, Council and World* (New York, 1963); Michael Serafian: *The Pilgrim* (New York, 1964). For an accurate story of the facts at the IInd Vatican Council, see Antoine Wenger: *Vatican II* (vol. I, Paris, 1963; vol. II, 1964; vol. III, 1965; vol. IV, 1966). For a perceptive Protestant appreciation of the doctrinal issues, see G. C. Berkouwer: *The Second Vatican Council and the New Catholicism* (Grand Rapids, Mich., 1965).

V.

The Church and the Kingdom

THE ECCLESIOLOGY of Vatican II could be approached from the standpoint of the traditional marks of the Church as listed in the Creed, one, holy, catholic, apostolic. The oneness of the Church is seen in the perspective of her mystery, by which the visible and the invisible are one. Her catholicity is the universality, in potentiality, in hope, and in fact, of the People of God. Her apostolicity is perceived in the continuity of the apostolic mission in the succession of the bishops. Thus, by successively treating of the Mystery, the People of God, and the hierarchy, the Council has surveyed three of the qualities under which the Church is essentially seen by the faithful. Only the quality, or mark, of holiness, however, is treated directly and at length.

"The Church, whose mystery is proposed by this Sacred Synod, is believed to be indefectibly holy" (art. 39). This indefectible holiness of the Church does not belong to her members, but, properly speaking, to Christ, who is, in the words of the Creed, "alone holy," as the Council reminds us immediately after the preceding quotation. The Church is holy; and holiness may be— nay, must be—predicated of her, though only on account of

Christ's abiding presence as the Head in the Body, as the groom with the bride, as the vine in the branches, or in any of the ways suggested by the biblical metaphors, in which Christ himself is presented as the source, the subject, and even the substance of the Church's holiness. This holiness consists in the Church being united to Christ, neither as a result of her efforts nor as a reward for merits that she could have gained or that somehow could be attributed to her. Rather, Christ's utterly gratuitous gesture of uniting the Church to himself in fidelity and love creates the Church's essential holiness. "For Christ," as the conciliar document explains it, "the Son of God, who, with the Father and the Spirit, is called alone holy, loved the Church like his own bride, giving himself for her in order to sanctify her, united her to himself like his own body, and filled her with the gift of the Spirit for the glory of God" (art. 39).

The first quality of the Church, in the Catholic frame of reference, identifies her as the realm of the numinous. The "sacred," which has been so much and so ably studied in recent years in its non-Christian manifestations, is embodied, for the Catholic mind, in the Church. The Church is the sacred as emanating from God through the incarnation of the Word. The perception of the Church's holiness goes back to the experience recorded in the Gospel of St. John in the words: "The Word was made flesh, and we have seen his glory, the glory as of the only-begotten, full of grace and of truth" (Jn. 1:14). The Church is the glory of the only-begotten. She is the *kabod* or *shekinah* of the Old Testament, that was perceived by the prophets and dwelt in the Temple. She is the halo or aura of created holiness that surrounded the Lord in the form of a cloud on Mount Tabor and of the healing power that restored the sick to health. She is the New Jerusalem revealed to the seer of the Apocalypse as already descending from heaven, the City that needs no Temple and no specific expression of holiness because the Lamb is himself her Temple and all in her incarnates holiness.

These expressions should open an insight into the Catholic belief in the Church's essential and superessential holiness. That she is a mystery, the mystery of Emmanuel, of God with man, makes her essentially numinous. That she is the holy People of the Lord, entrusted with his new and eternal covenant, presents another dimension of her holiness. That she is a hierarchy implies that the function of the sacred in her is never without celebrants, hierarchs in the fundamental sense of the expression. The Church protects and teaches the Holy Scriptures which she interprets according to her holy Tradition. The Councils are more than gatherings of men; they are "sacred synods." And the customs that are formed in her age after age are not simply "traditions of men," as the 16th-century Reformers thought: even when their history may be traced back to some event in the past and when they by no means proceed from the apostles or the early Fathers, they remain "holy traditions," unveiling a fundamental holiness.

All these avenues of approach to the Church's essential holiness point to the important fact—which should be held in mind whenever we speak of the holiness of the Church in a Catholic context—that holiness is, in and for the Church, an eschatological reality. The Christian experience of the numinous, the experience of awe before the "fearsome and fascinating" presence of God, amounts to much more than the feeling of awe obtained at the natural level or even at the level of the great world religions. It is more than a perception of the abyss separating men from the infinitely small or the infinitely great. It is awe before the face of God. Its two typical expressions in Judeo-Christianity are provided by the prophetic experience recorded by the great prophets of the Old Testament, and by the mystical experience alluded to by St. Paul: "I know a man in Christ who, fourteen years ago—was it in his body? I know not; was it outside of his body? I know not; God knows—this man was taken up to the third heaven. And this man—was it in his body or outside of his body? I know not; God knows—was taken up to Paradise and heard unutterable words, that cannot be pronounced by man" (2 Cor. 12:1–4).

The prophetic experience initiates a man to his function as prophet: he is called and made to speak for God, awed by his own mission:

"Before I formed you in the womb I knew you, and before you were born I consecrated you; I appointed you a prophet to the nations." Then I said, "Ah, Lord God! Behold, I do not know how to speak, for I am only a youth." But the Lord said to me, "Do not say, 'I am only a youth'; for to all to whom I send you you shall go, and whatever I command you you shall speak." [Jer. 1: 5–7]

Its sequel is enlightenment and obedience, fulfillment of the mission received, whatever odds may be against it. The mystical experience initiates into the intimate life of the Godhead, revealing "what eye has not seen and ears have not heard" (1 Cor. 2:9). Its sequel is an unavoidable and ineffable interior transformation toward a deeper realization of the "image and likeness" of God, which the Church Fathers called the deification of man.

* * *

Since these two basic types of Christian holiness will be infinitely diversified in their concrete realizations according to each man's specific call and grace, it is evident that the Council had to adopt another approach to Christian holiness than a mere description. Because of its pastoral purpose and scope, it proceeded from the fundamental holiness of the Church (art. 39) to the general call of all the faithful to holiness (art. 40), and to various forms of holiness adapted to the various functions of pastors, priests, clerics, married persons, workers and those who are afflicted with sufferings (art. 41). Throughout this exposition, one may, however, discern the two basic types of Christian holiness, prophetic and mystic, or, in more scholastic terms, the holiness of *gratia gratis data* and that of *gratia sanctificans,* that of function and that of transformation. Thus, all, "whatever their state or their order, are called to the fulness of Christian life and the perfection of love" (art. 40). All must be made "conform to his image" (*ibid.*). Holiness is reached by each "according to his own gifts and talents by way of a live faith, which inspires hope and works through love" (art. 41). Priests are exhorted to "ascend to a higher sanctity through their apostolic works, nourishing and fostering their actions with the abundance of their contemplation" (*ibid.*). Married persons are shown "following their own way in faithful love, all their life sustaining each other in grace" (*ibid.*). All, in brief, should "show to all, even in their temporal service, the love with which God loved the world" (*ibid.*).

One may wonder at this point how one passes from the essential holiness of the Church, which is indefectible and cannot be, properly speaking, achieved, since it is freely given by the Spirit, to the sanctity of the virtues which Christian life develops. One should avoid Pelagianism or even Semi-Pelagianism, condemned at the IInd Council of Orange (529), and incompatible with the decree of the Council of Trent on justification (session VI, 1547;

D.S., 1520–1583), and also the false mysticism that would simply equate the numinous power inherent in the Church with the sanctity of each believer. This passage is made clear in the last section of Chapter V: it is effected by participation—which is not achieved by merit but given by grace—in the charity of God "poured in our hearts by the Holy Spirit who has been given to us" (art. 42). The sacraments—especially the Holy Eucharist—prayer, self-renunciation and mutual service are both seeds and expressions of this love. Martyrdom is described as the scriptural and traditional high point of Christian holiness. The practice of the evangelical counsels and especially of holy virginity is mentioned as "a sign and incentive of love and a similar source of spiritual fecundity in the world" (art. 42).

I noted above that Christian holiness is essentially eschatological, implying a participation in the substantial holiness of the Church and the experience of the descending Kingdom in which God is all in all; it therefore anticipates the final return of all things to the Father through Jesus Christ in the Holy Spirit. It is a Trinitarian experience intimately depending on the indwelling of the Trinity in the Christian and the corresponding indwelling of the Christian in God. On the one hand, the Christian may say with St. Paul: "It is not I, but Christ who lives in me" (Gal. 2.20); on the other he may also repeat the words of the same apostle: "Our conversation is in heaven" (Phil. 3:20) and: "In him we move, and live, and have our being" (Acts 17:28), giving these words a fuller and truer sense than that of the speech at the Areopagus. The sum total of this prospective orientation of Christian holiness appears in these lines of the constitution *De Ecclesia:* "All the faithful of Christ are invited to strive for the holiness and perfection of their proper state . . . let them heed the admonition of the apostle to those who use this world; let them not come to terms with this world; for the world, as we see it, is passing away" (art. 42). The shape of this world passes away. Thus the faithful are on the way, pilgrims on a transient stage, toward a city not made with hands, to which they already belong, and the shape of which they anticipate in the insights of loving contemplation.

* * *

As it is lived in this life, Christian eschatology is an expectation which is progressively transformed, through the experience and the sacraments of faith, into an anticipation. The Christian expects the consummation of all things, their transformation in Christ, the manifestation of the children of God, the advent of a new heaven and a new earth, the appearance of the New Jerusalem, the return of Christ as the Son of man on the clouds of heaven to receive dominion over all and to judge the living and the dead. As St. Paul teaches, it is not only the Christian who looks forward to this consummation; but creation also expects it, waiting in travail for the manifestation of the children of God (Rom. 8:19). As he thought, at least when he was writing his letters to the Thessalonians, this expectation need not be long. Soon, the *parousia* will be celebrated, Christ returning at the sound of the trumpet, in the twinkling of an eye, and being acclaimed as Lord, to the glory of God the Father, the earth giving him the dignity which is already his in heaven. Catholic theology, in its scholastic formulation, has seen the virtue of hope as expressing this forward tension of the faithful, their orientation toward a world to come in which "God will wipe away all tears from their eyes," where "there will be no death, no tears, no cries, no sorrows, for the old world has passed away" (Apoc. 21:4). And the Catholic concept and practice of the liturgy regards worship here below as a communion with the worship of God by the Church in heaven. Those who give glory to God in this life act jointly with the "immense crowd" of the saints in heaven who proclaim: "Hail to our God, who sits on the throne, and to the Lamb" (Apoc. 7:10), and with the angels who sing: "Amen. Praise, glory, wisdom, thanksgiving, honor, power and strength to our God forever and ever. Amen" (Apoc. 7:12).

There have been saints, in the course of the Church's history, who sensed this expectation more than others and placed it at the center of their life: Origen, inviting the faithful to "destroy Jericho" in their hearts and thereafter to "sing the song of jubilation, for the world is destroyed and fallen for you";[1] Cistercian spirituality, urging the monks to reach "always toward the things ahead of us"; St. Thomas, defining the object of hope as "the infinite good, proportional to the power of God who gives it," that is, "God himself," for one "should not expect less of him than himself";[2] St. John of the Cross, in his poem *La Llama de Amor Viva,* exclaiming: "Rend the veil which stands in the way of our sweet encounter"; John Henry Newman, expressing in these terms the difference he saw between Old Testament and New Testament eschatology: "So it was that up to Christ's coming in the flesh, the course of things ran straight toward that end, nearing it by every step; but now, under the Gospel, that

1. *Homélies sur Josué,* Paris, 1960, p. 202.
2. *Summa Theologica,* II II, q. 17, a. 2.

course has, if I may so speak, altered its direction, as regards his second coming, and runs, not toward the end, but along it and on the brink of it; and it is at all times equally near that great event, which, did it run toward it, would run at once into it";[3] and a "great cloud of witnesses," who, more than those of the Old Testament of whom the Epistle to the Hebrews speaks, walked by faith toward "the leader of our faith, who leads it to perfection, Jesus ..." (12:2).

Not only are the Catholic notion of holiness and the corresponding practice of piety radically eschatological, Catholic theology and especially its reading of Scripture are also dominated by the Church's orientation toward the passing away of the world and the fulfillment of all things in Christ. As has been shown, more thoroughly than ever before, in Henri de Lubac's long study of medieval exegesis,[4] the key to Catholic, and not only medieval, reading of the Bible is the eschatological promise of the Spirit who "will guide you into all the truth" (Jn. 16:13). In so far as the Spirit is already given, one can read Scripture in the sense of the Spirit, through and beyond the letter whose meaning is available to the resources of scientific linguistics. The literal or historical sense provides an opening toward the spiritual meaning, which alone brings the Scriptures to their fulfillment in the soul. This is the anagogical sense, which crowns the reading of the Bible after the allegorical and the tropological senses have revealed some of the depths hidden in and by the literal sense.[5]

3. *Parochial and Plain Sermons,* vol. VI, p. 241.
4. *Exégèse Médiévale,* 4 vols., Paris, 1959–1964.
5. See "The Meaning of Scripture," in Leonard Swidler (ed.): *Scripture and Ecumenism,* Pittsburgh, 1965, pp. 59–73.

In so far as all Catholic theology originates in this traditional reading of the Scriptures, it in turns takes on a radically eschatological tone. For this reason, Pope Paul VI's encyclical *Ecclesiam Suam* insisted that the theology of the Church cannot be only a matter of reflection but depends also on experience: the question "will appear clearly, once the Church's own life is known by an experience illustrated and confirmed by the light of doctrine." It is significant that the questions which the Pope had in mind in this text refer to the tension between the Church's two aspects: "Why the Church must be held to the visible and spiritual, free and bound to a discipline, having the nature of a community and organized according to the degrees of a sacred hierarchy, already holy and nonetheless always striving after holiness, giving herself to contemplation and also to the active life."[6] These questions arise from the eschatological tension of a reality which lives in this world while it is not of this world. Such a tension cannot be known by way of speculation only; it is not the result of scientific conclusions and is not arrived at by syllogistic constructions. It is known in "the sense of the Church," which inspires an "excellent form of piety nourished by reading the Sacred Letters, the Fathers and the Doctors of the Church." This "form of piety" implies catechetical instruction, "active participation in the sacred liturgy. . . , silent and fervent meditation of heavenly truths, generous activity grounded in the pursuit of contemplation." This "study of Christian perfection must be considered as the best source where the Church draws her spiritual strength; as the proper way and the method to receive the lights of the Spirit of Christ faithfully; as the native and necessary

6. *Ecclesiam Suam*, Vatican Press, 1964, p. 21.

form in which the religious and social action of the Church is expressed; as the most certain support and the cause of her ever renewed strength in the difficulties of this profane world."[7] Thus the Church and the Church's thought point to that which they are not yet, although they partake of it in anticipation, namely to the future Kingdom of God coming down from heaven; the visible looks to the spiritual, the earthly to the heavenly, the pilgrim Church to the triumphant Church.

In these conditions, the Council's emphasis on eschatology in the constitution *Lumen Gentium* should not come as a surprise. Contemporary ecclesiology had prepared this for a long time by meditating on the mystery of the Church. The approach adopted by the Council itself prepared it by taking the "mystery" as its starting point, so that the internal chapters of the constitution seem, as it were, caught between a mysteric opening and an eschatological consummation, between an exposé of the mystery of Christ and his Bride at the beginning, and an evocation of the *parousia* and its anticipation in the Virgin Mary at the end. For eschatology as the explicit theme of the constitution is not only prominent in the seventh chapter ("The Eschatological Nature of the Pilgrim Church and Its Union With the Church in Heaven"); it also dominates the Mariological chapter which brings the constitution *Lumen Gentium* to an end.

* * *

That the Council introduces eschatology from the standpoint of the Church's essential holiness should not be forgotten. For this holds the key to the meaning of the text and to the vista which

7. *Ibid.*

116

the Council should open for a theology of the Church. "The Church, to which we are called in Jesus Christ and in which we acquire holiness by the grace of God, will attain its full perfection only in the glory of heaven, when the time comes for the restoration of all things" (art. 48). This introduction and a brief reminder of the function of Christ, drawing all things to himself and bringing mankind to salvation, lead to an important passage:

Already the final age of the world has come upon us, and the renovation of the world is irrevocably decreed and is already anticipated in some way; for the Church already on this earth is marked with a holiness which is real although imperfect. However, until there shall be new heavens and a new earth in which justice dwells, the pilgrim Church in her sacraments and institutions, which pertain to this present time, has the appearance of this world which is passing, and she herself dwells among creatures which groan and travail in pain until now and await the revelation of the sons of God. [art. 48]

Like others that could be quoted from the same chapter, this text contains no allusion to the widely advertised controversy over "future" or "realized" eschatology. This discussion has had little echo in Catholic theology, for reasons that are easy to see. On the one hand, Catholic theology is not so immediately affected by the latest theories about the interpretation of the New Testament as Protestant theology is. Thus the suggestion that Jesus and his immediate disciples would have adhered to a concept of future eschatology or that on the contrary they would have believed that, with the coming of the Messiah, eschatology was already being realized, can have little consequences for Catholic thought. What matters is not how modern exegetes read the Gospels, but how the Church's tradition, over the ages, has understood them. The details of contemporary exegesis are of less consequence than the broad consensus of the past in reading the New Testament, even if this consensus was more pastoral in purpose than scientific. On the other hand, the very notion of the Church as the only channel of sacramental grace, as the basic mystery of God's presence among men, as a unity of visible institution and invisible grace, as a synthesis of action and contemplation, as a union of the divine and the human, in a word, as a theandric society pursuing the divinization of man by incorporation into the Mystical Body of the Incarnate Lord, escapes the dichotomy between realized and future eschatology. For Catholic thought, future and realized eschatologies are neither contradictory nor exclusive. Far from it, they are mutually correlative, for the *eschaton* is future in so far as it is not yet entirely upon us; yet it would not be the *eschaton* for us unless it was already somehow upon us. The wave of the future for which the Church waits in eager expectation has already left the trace of its shape upon the visible realities of the Church. For what contemplation sees, what prophecy announces, what mystical grace reveals, what faith experiences and begins to understand, is the inchoation, the beginning, the first delineation of eschatology. Thus the Kingdom of God is both present and yet not totally so in the Church; the second coming is taking place, yet not finalized, in the sacraments; the vision is anticipated, yet not exhausted, in faith; the glory is dimly discerned in grace. An exaggeration of the presence of glory leads to a theology of glory without a corresponding theology of the cross; and the sense of the triumphant Church without the corresponding sense of the suffering Church leads to the "triumphalism" that was so

118

often denounced in the debates of the Ecumenical Council. In this spirit, the Council emphasizes the two aspects of eschatological dialectics: "Joined with Christ in the Church and signed with the Holy Spirit who is the pledge of our inheritance, truly we are called and we are sons of God, but we have not yet appeared with Christ in glory, in which we shall be like to God, since we shall see Him as He is" (art. 49).

The Christian, and the Church, strive therefore, in the exile of this life, to be faithful to the first-fruits of the Spirit. St. Paul's doctrine in the eighth chapter of the Epistle to the Romans dominates this passage which is deeply scriptural and profoundly traditional. The Christian life is agonistic, and we wear "the armor of God," entertaining a constant vigilance, "for we know not the day or the hour." The aim and purpose of life is the marriage feast of heaven, a reign with Christ in glory. The faithful, aware of the orientation of their life toward the fulfillment of all things in Christ at the end of the world, and living in hope, look forward to the ultimate revelation of the glory of God and to the transformation of their sinful humanity in conformity with the glorious humanity of the resurrected and ascended Christ: "Reckoning therefore that the sufferings of the present time are not worthy to be compared with the glory to come that will be revealed in us, strong in faith we look for the blessed hope and the glorious coming of our great God and Saviour, Jesus Christ, who will refashion the body of our lowliness, conforming it to the body of his glory, and who will come to be glorified in his saints and to be marveled at in all those who believed" (art. 48). From a literary point of view, this is little more than a catena of scriptural texts; from a theological standpoint, however, it expresses the core of the Christian message to

119

a world caught in a growing perplexity about the meaning of life and the limits of the universe of man.

The Christian is thus related to a heavenly reality not yet fully revealed. This is the "heavenly Church," as described in article 49 of the constitution *Lumen Gentium.* The total Church is made of three parts, "until the Lord comes in his majesty and all the angels with him and, death being destroyed, all things are subject to him"; for some of the faithful still pursue their earthly pilgrimage, some, "deceased from this life, are being purified," and others still are "in glory, seeing clearly God himself, Three and One, as he is." Thus the three stages of life according to the Catholic tradition are briefly enumerated: earth, purgatory and heaven. The thrust of the description, however, lies in the unity rather than the distinction of these levels of the Church. The faithful on earth, those who are being purified in preparation for the vision of God, and those who have already been admitted into the Holy of Holies do not constitute three assemblies of God, but only one: "All who are in Christ, having his Spirit, form one Church and cleave together in him." This point is of importance to understand Catholic eschatology.

The core of this eschatology is the expectation of Christ and the anticipation of his final advent in his present coming into the soul through faith and the sacraments of faith. But there is not simply a linear relationship to a future Christ, corresponding somehow to a linear relationship to the past Jesus of history. Our relationship to Christ is, actually, fan-wise, the fan being, so to say, fully open like a rainbow reaching from the horizon on one side to the horizon on the other side. Christ is at the start of the diameter at the bottom of the fan and he is also at the end of it on the far side: his historical advent on earth and his final advent in mankind as a whole and in the faithful soul mark the two basic extreme points of our relationship to him. Yet Christ stands also at all the points of the semi-circle formed by the open fan: he is there in himself by the presence of his Spirit and in the universality of his words, which attain "from one end of the horizon unto the other"; and he is also there in his angels and in his saints. The Catholic sense of eschatology implies a universal fraternity among all who have lived in Christ, who live in him today or who will live in him in the future. From this point of view, the Church is not a historical institution with a past and a future meeting at the fleeting moment of the present; she is rather a totality, permanent and stable, already at rest and beyond judgment. Within it, however, perpetual exchanges among the elect, those who are being purified and those who are being tested, establish dynamic links from the realm of glory to that of rest in the Lord and that of grace; there are strong bonds between eternity, *aevum* or "aeveternity," and time. "Therefore," the Council declares, "the union of the wayfarers with the brethren who have gone to sleep in the peace of Christ is not in the least weakened or interrupted, but, on the contrary, according to the perpetual faith of the Church, is strengthened by communication of spiritual goods." In the Christian universe, death is not a catastrophe and introduces no separation; it does not break established links and does not put asunder what God has united. Death is the passage from one state or level of life to another. It is the dynamic and profound experience of awakening to a new life, to the further development of the seeds of glory placed in the faithful at Baptism and grown up with the maturing of faith and the increase of sacramental life.

For this reason, Catholic piety is deeply eschatological even in its practice of prayer to and with the saints, who, because they are "more united with Christ, establish the whole Church more firmly in holiness." It would be absurd, for the Catholic mind, to think that all relations with those who have died in the Lord came to an end with their death. On the contrary, the scale of communication between this life and the next is traveled, like the scale of Jacob, both ways. In the first place, it is good and pious to pray for the dead. For, as the second Book of Maccabees, which is recognized as canonical in the Catholic Church, records it of Judas Maccabee, "It would have been foolish and superfluous to pray for the dead, if he had not believed that the fallen soldiers would resurrect; but if he believed that an excellent reward was reserved to those who sleep in piety, it was a holy and pious thought" (12:44–45). The Council quotes the last part of this citation in the Latin Vulgate translation: "It is a holy and pious thought to pray for the dead, that they may be loosed from their sins" (art. 50). In the second place, the dead themselves, holy souls in the sojourn of purification or saints in heaven, pray for those who are still being tested along the ways of their earthly pilgrimage.

This spiritual exchange among Christians includes the past, the present and the future, earth, purgatory and heaven, in one communion of saints. No one therefore ever prays alone; the whole Church is always present with, and assisting, those who pray. This is the eschatological meaning of the practise of prayer to—or, as we had rather say—*with* the saints, which the Council warmly recommends. "Fully conscious of this communion of the whole Mystical Body of Jesus Christ, the pilgrim Church from the very first ages of the Christian religion has cultivated with great piety the memory of the dead" (art. 50). The Council makes a short historical survey of this aspect of Christian piety, which is so striking in the paintings of the Roman catacombs and in the cult of the martyrs in the early Church. Admittedly, there may be abuses in devotion to saints, if it ever comes to push aside devotion to the Lord. This the Council wants to avoid by insisting on the eschatological implications of the communion of saints: "When we look at the lives of those who have faithfully followed Christ, we are inspired with a new reason for seeking the city that is to come." Through the saints, Christ speaks to us and draws us to himself: "In the lives of those who, sharing our humanity, are however more perfectly transformed into the image of Christ, God vividly manifests his presence and his face to men. He speaks to us in them, and gives us a sign of his Kingdom, to which we are strongly drawn, having so great a cloud of witnesses over us and such a witness to the truth of the Gospel" (art. 50). We should expect that these texts will orient Catholic piety to the saints in a more Christological direction than has at times been the case. Yet the focussing of true devotion on the central mystery of faith does not imply a de-emphasis of the meaning of holiness: holiness is an eschatological experience. A saint is a Christian who has been made by God a living icon of the coming Kingdom of God, and through whom the pilgrim Church reads some of the signs of the coming Kingdom.

For the pilgrim Church, looking forward to the Kingdom, is assisted by the Spirit to discern the signs of the time which herald the return of the Messiah. All the activities and meditations of the faithful may include this reference to the transcendent and to the future fulfilment of our hopes. Yet one specific Christian experience provides the best locus for our anticipation of the end, when heaven and earth shall pass away and the Word of the

Lord will remain eternally, thus creating a new heaven and a new earth in which Christians will, with the apostles, "sit on twelve thrones, judging the twelve tribes of Israel" (Lk. 22:30):

> Our union with the Church in heaven is put into effect in its noblest manner especially in the sacred liturgy, wherein the power of the Holy Spirit acts upon us through sacramental signs. . . . Then all those from every tribe and tongue and people and nation who have been redeemed by the blood of Christ and gathered together in one Church, with one song of praise magnify the one and triune God. [art. 50]

In other words, the liturgy provides the Church with an occasion on which the pilgrim Church rises above her pilgrim state and already shares the heavenly function of praise and the contemplation of the Holy Trinity. There, the communion of sacred things and the unity of all the faithful are achieved in all reality. For, as the *Apocalypse* of St. John eloquently shows it, there is only one liturgy in heaven and on earth. Significantly, it is on a quote from the *Apocalypse* that this chapter ends. Our union in the Pilgrim Church implies "a foretaste of the liturgy of consummate glory. For when Christ shall appear and the glorious resurrection of the dead shall take place, the glory of God shall light up the heavenly City and the Lamb will be the lamp thereof. Then the whole Church of the saints in the supreme happiness of love will adore God and the Lamb who was slain, proclaiming with one voice: To him who sits upon the Throne and to the Lamb, blessing and honor and glory and dominion for ever and ever" (Apoc. 5:13–14).

* * *

The eschatological destiny of the Church and its anticipation in the Christian life implies the possibility of being given already, in our pilgrim state, signs and icons of the Kingdom to come. It is now time to speak of two such signs which, although not entirely absent from Protestant Christianity, cannot receive in a Protestant context the emphasis which they have been traditionally given in Catholic life and thought. Both are explained at some length in the constitution *Lumen Gentium,* where they found acceptance, in their present form, after some hesitancies and difficulties.

The first is set in Chapter VI, between the chapter on the "call to holiness" and that on the eschatological vocation of Christians, two topics which, as I have explained, belong together as one. It is not by accident or as the result of strange maneuvers that the chapter on "religious Orders" is given this directly eschatological place in the constitution. For the religious life does not make sense unless it is seen in direct relation with the eschatological fulfillment of Christianity. The religious life consists, in canonical terms, in living according to a rule of life officially recognized as consecrated to God, usually by the three vows of poverty, chastity and obedience. It is the modern heir to the eremitical life of the early Church and the monastic life of the Middle Ages. The forms of religious life have obviously changed through the centuries, and there is little outside likeness between the members of a so-called "secular institute" of today and the desert Fathers of the 3rd century in Egypt. As it has changed in the past, the religious life is likely to change also in the future, as the Church brings her exterior forms and her theology in line with the pastoral requirements of each period. In spite of this fluent nature of the religious institution, the Fathers of the Vatican Councils have deemed it important to speak of it in the very center of the Council's preoccupation, namely in the constitution *De Ecclesia*. The reason for this lies in the close relationship of religious consecration with the two topics of holiness and eschatology.

"Since the evangelical counsels tie their followers to the Church and her mystery in a special way by the love to which they lead, their spiritual life must be devoted to the good of the whole Church" (art. 44). It is not its consecration as such which gives value to the religious life, but the charity which this consecration inspires. Thus the accent does not stress the canonical status of religious Orders and congregations, but their insertion in the life of charity of the Church. Yet there is more to the religious life than an occasion of greater love. And it is by no means suggested here that the so-called counsels of perfection which, in the New Testament, point up the dimension of self-transcendence in all Christian life, are reserved to those who take vows. The fact that the way of life of some members of the People of God is defined in relation to them, never implies that others of the faithful are exempt from also pursuing perfection in their life. Rather, the consecration of some to the service of God by the official endorsement of their vows of poverty, chastity and obedience acts as an image, for the whole Church, of the ultimate fulfillment to which all are called. In the terms of the Council itself: "The profession of the evangelical counsels appears as a sign which can and should attract all the members of the Church to an effective and prompt fulfillment of the functions of their Christian vocation. Since the People of God has no permanent city here below, but seeks a future city, the religious state, which gives its followers more freedom from earthly cares, manifests more fully to all believers the presence in this life of heavenly realities, it witnesses to the new and eternal life acquired by the redemption of Christ, and it foretells the resurrection to come and the glory of the heavenly Kingdom" (art. 44).

This theological description of the religious life, which completes its canonical definition according to the notions of consecrated life, of counsels of perfection and of vows, sees the meaning of the religious life in the line of what was called above the prophetic type of holiness. The religious, today as in the past, are prophets, whose lives should be parables of the Kingdom of God. Admittedly, institutional prophecy, now as in the Old Testament, is always a dangerous venture. There may be false, bad or simply lukewarm prophets. But the scope of the Council's declaration on this particular sign of the Kingdom of God should be taken in a positive way, as an incentive to restore the religious life to its truly prophetic and eschatological dimension.[8]

* * *

More importance still is given to the theme of the Virgin Mary in the last chapter of the constitution. One will not understand this if it is read as a compromise between Mariological tendencies, which would have agreed on a happy medium or on some sort of common denominator, avoiding maximalism and minimalism as two excesses. It may be more difficult to read this chapter without bias, mainly because we are still too near to the debates of the Council, and we lack the perspective and the

8. On this topic, see *The Church Tomorrow,* ch. 5, "Reform of the Religious Life through the Liturgy."

detachment necessary to assess the scope of conciliar documents. Yet the lines indicating the relevance of Mary to a theology of the Church are clearly marked in the text.

Mary is "a type and an excellent exemplar" of the Church "in faith and in love" (art. 53); she is, "for all the community of the elect, the model of virtues" (art. 65); she is "a type of the Church in the order of faith, of love and of perfect union with Christ" (art. 63); "in the mystery of the Church, who is rightly called mother and virgin," she is "eminently and singularly the exemplar of the mother and the virgin" (art. 63). These expressions do not exhaust the constitution's suggestions about Mary; and since the Council did not wish to end theological investigations, it could not adopt one approach only to the mystery of the Mother of God, but it had to combine several. The one which, from the point of view of this book, seems the most fruitful is the typological approach. For, whatever the merits of other theologies, this one has the advantage of setting the contemplation of Mary within the mystery of Christ and the Church. Mary is a sign of salvation, an icon representing the Church at her best for our hope and our consolation, an anticipation of what not only the Church as a whole, but all Christian souls, are also destined to be at the consummation of the Kingdom of God. Mary is mother and virgin. The Church also, as the Council, following an important stream of Catholic Tradition, assures us, is mother and virgin:

The Church, contemplating her hidden holiness, imitating her love, faithfully fulfilling the Father's will, is also made mother by the word of God which she faithfully receives: by preaching and Baptism she begets children, conceived of the Holy Spirit and born of God, to the new and immortal life. And she also is virgin, who keeps faith with her Spouse in integrity and purity . . . [art. 64][9]

Let us listen to the voice of the Catholic Tradition witnessing to its belief in the fulfilment of the eschatological consummation in the personal life of Christians, and in the birth of the Kingdom of God in the soul: "O eternal Word of the Father," Pope John XXIII exclaimed in his Christmas message for 1962, "renew once more in the hiddenness of the soul the admirable wonder of your birth."[10] This is a recent echo of the words of the Gospel, which the Catholic Tradition understands no less of Mary's actual holiness than of the possible holiness of all the faithful: "Who are my mother and my brothers? . . . He who does the will of God is my brother and my sister and my mother" (Mk. 3:33–35).[11]

This is the ultimate point of Catholic eschatology: in the Mother of God eminently and in all souls devoted to God imperfectly, the mystery of spiritual motherhood is fulfilled.[12] The Church, and Mary, and each of the faithful, are sister and mother to Christ. The Church universally, Mary historically and typi-

9. See Karl Delahaye, *op. cit.*

10. *La Documentation Catholique,* 1963, n. 1391, col. 6.

11. On the relevance of Mary to a theology of the Church, see Congar: *Le Christ, Marie et l'Eglise* (Bruges, 1962); Karl Rahner: *Mary, Mother of the Lord* (New York, 1963); Stanislas Cwiertniak: *La Vierge Marie dans la Tradition Anglicane* (Paris, 1958); Max Thurian: *Mary, Mother of All Christians* (New York, 1963).

12. See the admirable poem called "75th Prayer" by Gregory of Narek in Grégoire de Narek: *Le Livre de Prières,* Paris, 1961, pp. 391–410: ". . . This Mother, who is more spiritual, heavenly, luminous, —than earthly, breathing, corporeal, —has cared for me as for a son; —the milk from her breasts is the blood of Christ . . . —She is pregnant with created gods, —pure images of the one God, Christ . . ."

cally, all Christians singularly and mystically, constitute the meeting point of the earthly and the heavenly, the human and the divine, the historical and the eternal, mankind on pilgrimage and mankind in the new heaven and the new earth. This is the mystery of the Church and of the sacramental anticipation of its fulfillment, before which we must ultimately retire into the wondering silence of contemplation.

VI.

The Religious in the Church

1. The Council's Decree

LIKE ALL OTHER documents of the Council, the Decree on the Adaptation and Renewal of the Religious Life is to be read in the light of the doctrinal constitutions which embody the fundamental doctrines of Vatican II, and especially of the constitution *De Ecclesia,* which devotes an entire chapter to the religious Orders. The approach adopted in the constitution should therefore help us to determine our understanding of the Decree on Religious Life.[1]

Chapter VI of the Constitution on the Church is set between a chapter on the universal call to sanctity and one of the eschatological nature of the pilgrim Church and her union with the

1. On the topic of this chapter, see our *The Church Tomorrow,* ch. 5, "Reform of the Religious Life through the Liturgy." See also *Decree on the Adaptation and Renewal of the Religious Life,* with a Commentary by Gregory Baum, Glen Rock, 1966.

Church in heaven. After speaking, from Chapters III to IV, of the functional hierarchy (bishops, priests, deacons, laymen), the Council now considers the charismatic hierarchy. In several of his epistles, St. Paul lists various ministries in the Church, "apostles, prophets, teachers, powers, gifts of healing, helping, administration, kinds of tongues" (1 Cor. 12:28). In these enumerations, he usually puts together functional ministries and charismatic ones. But the subsequent history of the Church introduced a sharp cleavage between the official, institutional hierarchy in charge of government, based on the historical incarnation, and the charismatic hierarchy, based on the free gifts and inspirations of the Spirit. Whereas the institutional hierarchy provides a testimony to the depth of the incarnation, by which the Word became flesh and instituted a visible organism of his disciples, the charismatic hierarchy witnesses to the freedom of the Spirit, who doles out talents and calls to himself those whom he selects in the way which he chooses. Both hierarchies are essential to the Church.

The Vatican Council recognized the importance of the charismatic hierarchy by treating the question of holiness in the Church at length: the holiness to which all are called (Ch. V), the call to holiness embodied in the religious Orders (Ch. VI), the eschatological status of the Church, which lives both on earth and in heaven (Ch. VII), the fulfillment of the Church's holiness in the Virgin Mary, raised by God to the summit of the charismatic hierarchy (Ch. VIII).

The chapter on the religious proceeds from a consideration of the so-called evangelical counsels (art. 43), that is, of the spiritual dimension of the Gospel, to their implementation in the vows or other links of religious institutes (art. 44), then to the more practical and detailed organization of religious Orders, in which the charismatic hierarchy is controlled by the functional hierarchy (art. 45), and finally to the religious life as helping the Christian personality to reach fruition (arts. 46–47). In this necessarily brief outline, one point stands out with remarkable clarity: the existence of religious Orders, where the charisms of the Spirit are outwardly manifested by a special way of life and a unique vocation, belongs to the esthetic aspect of the Church's manifold diversity. Religious vocations are not to be understood only in terms of holiness, of service of the Church, or of spreading the Gospel, but also in terms of beauty. The Council speaks in this way:

The result [of the Spirit's guidance] has been as if a tree had grown from the seed God gave, and sent out its branches in striking manner in many quarters of God's field. There has come about the growth of different rules of life, solitary or in community, and of different families which multiply the resources for the improvement of their members and the good of the whole body of Christ. [art. 43]

And again:

Religious must make it their careful aim that their efforts improve the Church's real and daily exhibition of Christ as he meditates on the hillside, as he proclaims the Kingdom of God to the crowds, as he heals the sick and the injured, in his conversion of sinners toward goodness, in his blessing of children, in his doing good to all and in his continual obedience to the will of the Father who sent him. [art. 46]

The religious life belongs to the realm of the uncharted paths of the Spirit, who distributes calls and charisms as he sees fit. Yet, because it constitutes an epiphany, a showing forth of the ways of the Spirit, it also belongs to the essential beauty of the Body of Christ, in which Christ's own life is reflected in the attitude and the activities of the members of his Church.

Both charisms and spiritual beauty imply liberty. The charisms of the Spirit require the freedom to receive them, and their reception gives access to the realm of the higher liberty of the children of God. Insight into spiritual and theological beauty also entails the capacity, and therefore the freedom, to discern the beautiful from the ugly, the spiritual from the material; and awareness of beauty initiates into another realm of life, that of life in the Exemplar of all created beauty, the eternal Word of God, Uncreated, Incarnate and Infused into the world by the Spirit.

Thus we find that three notions are central to a consideration of the religious life in the Church: that of charism, that of beauty, that of liberty.

*　*　*

The decree on the Religious Life starts on a similar esthetic note:

From the very beginning of the Church, men and women have set about following Christ with greater freedom and imitating him more closely through the practice of the evangelical counsels, each in his own way leading a life dedicated to God. . . . So it is that in accordance with the divine plan a wonderful variety of religious communities has grown up, which has made it easier for the Church, not only to be equipped for every good work and ready for the work of the ministry, the building up of the Body of Christ, but also to appear adorned with the various gifts of her children like a bride adorned for her husband, and for the manifold wisdom of God to be revealed through her. [art. 1]

Here also we find the notion of freedom, that of charisms, or free gifts of the Spirit, and that of beauty.

134

The beauty in question has two aspects: simplicity and variety. On the one hand, it shows forth the simplicity of the Gospel. On the other, it inspires and creates a multiplicity of vocations, forms of life and ways in which the Gospel is spread and applied. There is "a great variety of gifts," yet one focus of religious life, the Lord Jesus. The Spirit attracts men in many varied ways, shows himself under many forms and speaks through many voices. Yet he leads to the one center of Christian life, the Redeemer, in the one Church which is the ark of salvation.

Accordingly, the renovation of religious life will have to keep two points of view together: the freedom of the Spirit, which has its counterpart in the freedom of the men and women whom he calls and endows with his gifts, and which is destined to end up in a rainbow of talents, charisms, initiatives, inspirations, achievements, spiritual traditions and perspectives; and the uniqueness of the center, whose image is reflected in the ascetic and mystical dimension of the Gospel, especially through what we call—with an unbiblical and somewhat misleading term— the counsels of perfection.

Because of the freedom of the Spirit, there are many forms of holiness and many varieties of religious life. The Council mentions those "which are entirely consecrated to contemplation" (art. 7), others given to "the works of apostolate" (art. 8), the monastic institutions (art. 9), the lay religious Orders (art. 10), the secular institutes (art. 11). This list is not restrictive, since the principle of freedom must play within each of these broad categories; and there will be a great variety of gifts and of forms of life and apostolate within each of these groups and even within each religious Order. We should devote some time to these descriptions, before considering the other aspect of religious vocation, the centrality of Christ.

The religious life is presented, in Article 5, as radically contemplative. "The members of every community, seeking God solely and before all else, must join contemplation, by which they adhere to him with their mind and their heart, to apostolic love, by which they will seek to be associated to the work of redemption and to spread the Kingdom of God." The Council thus takes it for granted that the soul of all religious life, personally and corporatley, that is, for each person and for each institute, is contemplation. This is not necessarily to be taken in the formal theological sense of the term, in which it denotes the reception of, and the fidelity to, mystical grace; yet it is obviously intended to have the general meaning of a theological vision, of a certain view of supernatural and natural realities, of a guiding principle of the spiritual order, in relation to which all other things fall into place and life appears to have meaning. This contemplation, this vision, this guiding light, is entirely relative to God, since it is the medium in which the religious mind adheres to Him. Adhesion to God being achieved through the theological virtues, the fundamental principle of a religious Order should lie in an oriented understanding and practice of faith, hope and love.

This contemplation will be joined to apostolic love, that is, to some commitment to public witness for the Kingdom of God, according to the requirements of time and place and to the particular needs of one's neighbors. Thus the two commandments of love for God and of love for neighbor, which are basically one according to the Gospel, will also be united in life. But it should go without saying that this junction of contemplation and action, which, according to the Constitution on Sacred Liturgy, Article 2, "belongs to the essence of the Church," should not result in an artificial appendage of practices of piety to a life of strenuous and dispersed activity, or, conversely, that it should not consist in tacking a few disjointed actions to a life of contemplative leisure. Rather, the one has to flow from the other. Contemplation inspires the type of action to be undertaken. Action collects, as it were, the overflow of one's personal vision of the supernatural world. That is to say, contemplation, which results from the free gifts of the Spirit and which introduces further into the liberty of the children of God, does not usually create conformity to a given pattern, even if this has been endorsed canonically by the Church's authorities. It will create originality, in the proper sense of the word: it will inspire strong personalities, able to carry out in practice what the Spirit will reveal to them in their inner vision and what he will suggest in his interior promptings. Thus the contemplation which the Council sees as the very basis of religious communities will be the source of "common unities," of the sharing in common of very diverse spiritual visions in a multitude of individuals. The ensuing common life will therefore never fall into any set pattern, but will move freely according to the requirements of the times and the gifts of those who share it.

In each special form of religious life envisioned, this should remain the leading principle of authority. Therefore, what the Council describes as being the contemplative life (art. 7), the apostolic life (arts. 8 and 10), the monastic life (art. 9), and the consecrated life of secular institutes (art. 11), can only be indicative of general tendencies rather than restrictive of the free initiatives of the Spirit. The principle of freedom, of charismatic vocation, of the beauty arising from the ordered contrasts and the complementarity of multiplicity, must be preserved within all religious Orders. For this reason, the Decree on Religious Life ascribes to the same sources the spiritual life of all of them, whatever their origin, their theology, their conception of their vocation and the organization of their common life:

> Let those who make profession of the evangelical counsels seek and love above all else God who has first loved us; and let them strive to foster in all circumstances a life hidden with Christ in God. . . . Drawing upon the authentic sources of Christian spirituality, members of religious communities should resolutely cultivate both the spirit and the practice of prayer. In the first place, they should have recourse daily to the Holy Scriptures, in order that, by reading and meditating on Holy Writ, they may learn 'the surpassing worth of knowing Jesus Christ.' They should celebrate the sacred liturgy, especially the holy sacrifice of the Mass, with both lips and heart, as the Church desires, and so nourish their spiritual life from the richest of sources. [Art. 6]

It is remarkable that what is mentioned in this paragraph applies to the life of all Christians. Love of God, life hidden with Christ in God, the Scriptures, liturgical participation in the sacrifice of Christ are by no means reserved to, or specific of, any religious Order. They belong to the common stock of the Church and are available and recommended to all the People of God. Admittedly, the Council also says that each religious Order ought to cultivate the spirit of its founders: "Let their founders' spirit and special aims which they set before them, as well as their sound traditions —all of which make up the patrimony of each institute—be faithfully held in honor" (art. 2). There is no reason not to extend this recommendation to the direction of the spiritual life which some founders have conceived as typical of their institute and to the several schools of spirituality which have sprung up in the wake of the major Orders. Yet it remains that ordinary Christian life and spirituality predominate, and that all that may be distinctive of one religious Order in the area of spiritual contemplation is a special ordering of the elements common to the whole Church, with the provision that personal attractions may vary considerably from the accepted norm of the Order. Here again, the focus on the ordinary means of Christian life rather than on the distinctive features of each spirituality helps to maintain the principle of freedom: the freedom of the Spirit, who distributes his charisms without being impeded by rules and regulations, and who thus creates beauty where men would only have put order.

Spiritual life has two poles: the Word and the sacraments, the Scriptures and the Eucharist, the *lectio divina* and the liturgy. Thus the Decree on the Renewal of Religious Life tallies with the Constitution on Revelation and with that on the sacred liturgy. It follows that religious Orders must, in keeping with the mind of the Council, assist their members in becoming both more scriptural in their thinking and their piety, and more liturgical in their participation in the sacraments. The Scriptures must cease to be a closed book, especially to many members of feminine congregations. Accordingly, the required instruction and initiation should be provided so that all may read the Scriptures, not simply as a source-book of data about Christ and the Church, and not at all as a text-book for apologetic argumentation, but as the Word of God written for their own edification. Likewise, the liturgy must cease to be an occasion for exercises of piety, in which private devotions—even if they are the private devotions of the founder of an Order and the collective official devotions of an Order—offset the primary importance of corporate worship.

* * *

If the religious life implies the freedom of the Spirit, it also has its sole center in the Incarnate Lord as he presents himself in the Gospel, that is, as a master who shows the way, because he *is* the way, who teaches all that he has heard from the Father, who, having been raised on the Cross, draws all men unto himself, who brings about the coming of the kingdom of God through the utter simplicity of his spiritual doctrine.

The traditional way of speaking of religious Orders, which is used again in our document, has focussed attention on the "counsels of perfection," that is, on recommendations or invitations made by Christ to those of his followers who would have the generosity to understand them, and to which the other disciples would supposedly not be bound. This is still the prevalent understanding of the counsels of perfection, a conception for which we would look in vain in the Scriptures themselves or among the Fathers of the Church, and which seems to have appeared rather late in the Middle Ages. Admittedly, much of the self-interpretation of the contemporary Orders has been built around it. Yet it implies a very questionable view of spiritual perfection.

Whereas both the Constitution on the Church and the Decree on Religious Life speak of the counsels of perfection, neither opposes them to the universally valid commandments. They speak of "those who profess the evangelical counsels" (art. 6). But there is no suggestion that the counsels are some sort of preserve, off bounds to the majority of the People of God. Mem-

Sister Mary David,

If you have time
read the chapter:
The Religious in
the Church —

SMS

bers of religious Orders, at least some of them, have officially pronounced the vows of poverty, chastity and obedience. Yet poverty, chastity and obedience are part and parcel of all Christian life. The Gospel does not present two "vehicles" or "ways," one for the ordinary majority and another for the select few. Until recently a distinction was clearly drawn between the religious Orders, defined by vows, and the unvowed laity. Yet this distinction clearly broke down when Pope Pius XII declared the vowless secular institutes to be also in the way of life defined by the counsels of perfection. Thus we are faced at this point, not, as before, with a principle of differentiation and variety, but with a unification of all Christian ethics, asceticism and mysticism in the stark simplicity of the image of Christ in the Gospel.

Chastity "for the Kingdom of God" (art. 12), "voluntary poverty for the sake of following Christ, of which it is a sign" (art. 13), obedience as "the offering of one's own will as a sacrifice to God" (art. 14), are not specific obligations applying to one set of Christians rather than to another. They are points of view from which the Gospel makes better sense. They are a way of life, not in so far as they distinguish some persons from others, but in as much as they penetrate the life of all. They are principles which inspire ascetic practices and throw light on the meaning of life with Christ. They are incentives to self-transformation for the kingdom of God and to self-dedication to the service of men. All Christians are called to practice them in their life, according to their circumstances and moral obligations, and in keeping with their sacramental graces and the gifts of the Spirit. They do not mark out one group of the faithful as being already "in a state of perfection," but all the faithful as seeking perfection together.

In relation to this fundamental truth of Christian spirituality, the ways in which the Orders have institutionalized chastity, poverty and obedience through vows or promises, through complicated hierarchies of authority within each Order, each province and even each house, through regular reports and accounts of their doings and of their needs and expenses, are of secondary importance. In contrast with the evangelical teaching concerning the desire for perfection, which does not pass away, the practical implementation of the vows in the rules and constitutions of religious Orders is an historical accident of relatively recent origin in the history of the Church; and it may at any time be brought into jeopardy by unforeseen circumstances which may make the survival of these institutions impossible. In this case, the Gospel would remain; and the relevance of all the commandments and counsels to all the faithful would always be valid.

If the principle of the freedom of the Spirit inspires diversity, the principle of the unique center, Jesus Christ, creates unity and unanimity. The beauty of which I spoke at the beginning results from the proportion of diversity and unity in the life of each of the faithful and in the relations of the faithful among themselves. The religious Orders are important elements in the ordering and the diversifying of life in the Body of the Church. From this standpoint, they belong to the esthetic aspect of catholicity. In the long run, this is of more value and importance than their canonical status, their traditional privileges, their tendency to parochialism and their desire to keep their identity among the other unities and diversities of the Church. The lasting sections of the Decree on the Renewal of Religious Life will presumably be those which will help to develop the constitutive factors of the esthetic relevance of religious Orders: charisms and freedom of the Spirit, as balanced against the unifying effect of Christ at the heart of the Church, —rather than the passages dealing with the canonical aspects of the religious life.

Yet it is to be expected that many readers will notice those canonical notes rather than the theology underlying the text. In practice, therefore, the Decree on Religious Lift, like many documents of many Councils, may become spiritual in the hands of mystics, theological in the hands of theologians, canonical in the hands of canonists, progressive in the hands of those who are for progress, conservative in the hands of those who are for conservation, freeing in the hands of those who trust the freedom of the children of God, oppressive in the hands of those who practice authoritarianism. Read, as it ought to be, in the context of the constitution *De Ecclesia* and in conjunction with the constitutions *De Liturgia* and *De Revelatione,* it forms a ready instrument for renewal. Even if it is not the best that could have been produced, it contains enough theological insights into the depths of the religious soul to render a far-reaching renovation of religious Orders feasible.

* * *

It seems to me that several questions are raised by the way I have read the Decree on the Religious Life. I am not referring to concrete problems of detailed organization or of precedure, but to fundamental questions regarding the nature and the future of religious Orders.

If it is true, and I believe it is, that the counsels of perfection are not specific of the religious vocation, that the vows themselves are not necessary to the religious life as officially recognized by the Church, that the spirituality of religious Orders is that of the Gospel, beyond what flourishes and embellishments have been developed in the course of a long ascetic and mystical tradition, that the two foci of religious life are the freedom of the Spirit and the centrality of the Word Incarnate, it would seem to follow that nothing is particularly typical of the religious life; and that there is no characteristic of religious Orders that could not also be predicated of Christian life as a whole. In these conditions, we may legitimately wonder what, if anything, belongs to religious Orders as such.

I would see the specific element of the religious life in the concept of community. The Council itself speaks of the common life in terms that are worthy of note:

Common life, fashioned on the model of the early Church where the body of believers was united in heart and soul, and given new force by the teachings of the Gospel, the sacred liturgy and especially the Eucharist, should continue to be lived in prayer and the communion of the same spirit. As members of Christ living together as brothers, religious should give pride of place in esteem to each other and bear each other's burdens. For the community, a true family gathered together in the name of the Lord by God's love which has flooded the hearts of its members through the Holy Spirit, rejoices because he is present among them. . . . The unity of the brethren is a visible pledge that Christ will return and a source of great apostolic energy. [art. 15]

Once again, the religious life has been described in terms which would perfectly fit the Church as a whole and many smaller Christian communities, especially that of the family, to which the religious community is explicitly compared. In other words, community life does not describe the religious life; but simply the Christian life lived according to the Gosepl. There recurs now the same law of identification with the whole Church

144

and with the life of the People of God which we have already met. What specifies the religious community is therefore not that it is a community, but that it is this particular concrete community, the association of such and such, with their peculiar vocations and gifts, their understandings of their function, their spiritual and natural individualities and personalities, their past, their dreams and their future, their qualities and their short-comings.

The specific element of each religious Order and each com-munity resides simply in those who form that Order or that community, just as the specific element distinguishing one family from another is simply the association of the persons who are bonded together in marriage. The common life, as described by the Council, does not essentially consist in living together under one roof and from one purse, but, on the image of the apostolic Church, in "union of heart and soul," in prayer and "the com-munion of the same spirit." In other words, it is not a shelter providing for the necessities of life, but the unity of a common purpose. It is therefore possible that, in certain circumstances, and given the personalities and the spiritual gifts of those who share in it, the common life will be less a living together than a banding together for mutual material and spiritual support. On the principle of the freedom of the Spirit, the common life can-not be the same for all, although, on the principle of the cen-trality of Christ, it must always be focussed on the manifestation of love for one another in the Lord. Yet, here again, the religious life has not been set apart from the life of the People of God: it is that very same life, lived analogously, by persons who have been called each in a unique way to the fulfillment of the Gospel.

It would seem, then, that, in ultimate analysis, the religious life should be destined to merge into the wider religious life of the People of God and the wider community of the Church. Certainly there will always be smaller units within the larger one, icons and images of the Body at a less than universal level. Yet the predominance of the elements that belong at the same time to the People of God and to the religious communities would tend to impose the conclusion that, the less different they appear to be, the better they will be able to fulfill their vocation. The ultimate point of spirituality is not to be isolated from the crowd, but to be a leaven in the crowd, sharing its hopes and its virtues and its problems and its sufferings. Likewise, the ultimate goal for a religious community is to be indistinguishable from the People of God, of which it is a living cell. This is, admittedly, the opposite of the ideal, sometimes presented to religious Orders, of separation from the world. Unfortunately, separation from the world—which is good if the world is taken to mean an epitome of evil—has also meant, in fact, separation from the People of God, separation from the Church. The religious habit has symbolized it and the enclosure has made it effective. This emphasis, I suspect, is destined to disappear in the future; and the sooner the better.

This brings in the last, and the most controversial, question. If religious Orders have nothing specific in themselves besides the personalities of their members; if their way of life is simply that of the Gospel, which ought to be, in any case, the way of life of all Christians; if what distinguishes a religious layman from a Catholic layman, and a religious priest from a diocesan priest, is simply the smaller cell in which he tries to achieve on a minor scale what the Church should be universally, one may wonder if the religious life is not destined, simply, to disappear.

Of course, the Council provides no guidance here, except the important point that it does expect religious Orders to continue at least long enough to read and begin to apply the Decree on the Renewal and Adaptation of Religious Life. It also provides the insight that, since the religious life belongs to the charismatic order, it may last as long as the charisms of the Spirit. Yet there is no guarantee that it shall last and that the charisms of the Spirit shall not inspire other forms of Christian commitment than those we have known. Some psychologists think that the religious life is doomed, because it would seem to evoke less and less response on the part of younger people, who find other religious and spiritual ideals more attractive. Some sociologists think that the classical forms of poverty and obedience are no longer workable in our world; and considerable evidence could be drawn to support this point. Yet this means only that other forms of the same principles will need to be discovered. The Council itself invites to such a search: "Religious should . . . if need be, express in new forms that voluntary poverty . . . [etc.] . . ." (art. 13).

Whether religious Orders will last will depend on their power of renewal. There is no justification for their continuance, if this means barely surviving like a sick body, artificially prolonging their existence by catching young people who could find the same or a better thing elsewhere. It will also depend on their imagination and their regrouping. There is no reason to multiply distinct Orders if the difference between them is only one of name and of origin. It will finally depend on their fidelity to the freedom of the Spirit and the centrality of the Word.

In the long run, the religious Orders do not matter. What matters is the freedom of the children of God which they exemplify, the charismatic gifts of the Spirit and the prophetic leaven which they keep before the eyes of the People of God, the charismatic hierarchy which complements the institutional hierarchy, the primacy of contemplation which they should foster, the beauty of the ever faithful yet ever changing Church of Christ, to which they contribute.

2. The Vows

In his address to all religious, pronounced on May 23, 1964, Pope Paul VI said: "It has seemed good to us to recall here the priceless importance and necessary function of religious life; for this stable way of life, which receives its proper character from profession of the evangelical vows, is a perfect way of living according to the example and teaching of Jesus. It is a state of life which keeps in view the constant growth of charity leading to its final perfection." The Pope adopted here the point of view of the authors who see the proper characteristics of the religious life in the profession of the evangelical vows, by which the determination to pursue the virtues and counsels of perfection is expressed and the imitation of Christ is fulfilled: "If you wish to be perfect, sell all that you have . . ." (Mt. 19:21). "There are eunuchs . . . who have made themselves so for the Kingdom of heaven. Let him understand who can" (Mt. 19:21). And finally the statement of the Epistle to the Hebrews on the obedience of Christ: "Son as he was, he learnt obedience through the things which he suffered" (Hebr. 5:8). That Pope Paul would use a

148

classical manner of speech, here as elsewhere, is quite in keeping with the function of the magisterium to preserve what is, until Christian reflection has found better ways of expressing and explaining the fundamental Christian intuition underlying the institutions of Christian life. The task still remains to interpret what is thus said and to read it in the perspective of an advancing theological tradition, rather than by reference to a static scheme set once for all times.

Our problem is now to understand the meaning of the three vows of obedience, chastity and poverty, or rather, from the point of view which I have adopted, the meaning of the three virtues which the vows are destined to promote. Not all religious pronounce vows, but all pursue the virtues; not all Christians are bound by vows, but all are bound by the corresponding virtues.

A theological conception of Christian life would find it inconceivable that Christian perfection should be focussed on what we call "moral virtues." Chastity, poverty, obedience, relate to behavior, to action, rather than to being and essence. Yet Christian perfection is surely in the first place a question of ontological transformation into the image of God on the pattern of Christ. Insistence on the importance of three particular forms of activity for those who wish to fulfill the commandment, "Be perfect as your Father in heaven is perfect" (Mt. 5:48), would be a subtle, or not so subtle, form of Pelagianism. Holiness does not reside in what we do, but in what we are. It is not the outcome of human determination and efforts, but of the grace and power of the Spirit. It does not result from a desire to be perfect and to follow the way of perfection, but from the transformation initiated by baptism and completed by the Holy Eucharist. Indeed, St. Teresa of Avila gave the name of "way of perfection," not to an exposé of the religious life, but a map of mystical contemplation, which is itself the flowering, in all Christian life, of the mystagogical experiences of baptism and the Supper of the Lord.

The three virtues that are central to Christian life and perfection are therefore not chastity, poverty and obedience, but the traditional theological virtues by which, as St. Thomas explains, man is directly oriented to God (II II, q. 17, a. 6, ad 2). Love, hope and faith, as they are described in the New Testament (love: 1 Cor. 13; hope: Rom. 8; faith: Hebr. 11) and understood in theology, effect man's transformation from a natural likeness to a supernatural image of God; they lead him from the land of dissemblance to the land of resemblance; they make him, a stranger, into a friend of God; they change his name from "Not-My-People" to "My-People" (Hos. 2:25). In them the Christian man experiences what the Gospel of John describes in these words: "Out of his fullness we have received all, grace upon grace" (Jn. 1:16). And the other St. John, John of the Cross, formulates their climax in this striking phrase: ". . . all the things of God and the soul are one in participating transformation. And the soul looks more like God than like a soul, and even is God by participation."[2] Accordingly, Christian perfection is the perfection of love, hope and faith. And if chastity, poverty and obedience make any sense in relation to the quest for perfection, this can only be insofar as they are nothing but love, hope and faith. Religious should not pronounce vows of chastity, poverty and obedience; they ought to vow love, hope and faith, because this is what chastity, poverty and obedience mean. They mean nothing else.

In the New Testament, the three virtues correspond to the

2. *Ascent of Mount Carmel,* bk. II, ch. 5, n. 7.

three "desires" of the First Epistle of St. John: "All that is in the world—the desire of the flesh, the desire of the eyes, the pride of wealth—does not come from the Father, but from the world" (1 Jn. 2:16). These in turn evoke the three temptations of Christ, whom the Devil tried to induce into a false conception of the nature of man (the temptation against faith, to which the answer is: "Man does not live by bread alone, but by every word coming from the mouth of God"), into a false relationship to creation (the temptation to magic, which binds spiritual and cosmic powers at the service of man), into a false conception of self (the temptation to be king). The first temptation is against the incarnation; it is overcome by faith, manifested in obedience. The third opposes the universal kingship of the Father; it is overcome by hope, manifested in self-dispossession or poverty. The second is against the Spirit, who "hovers over creation" (Gen. 1:2); it is overcome by love, manifested in chastity.

Chastity is to be understood in the perspective of love. Poverty makes sense in relation to hope. Obedience rests upon the reality of faith. Since the three theological virtues are not absolute, but radically relative to God as he has revealed himself in Christ, it is possible to see them as effecting a special unity with the three divine Persons. In the course of Christian life, God fulfills the promise made in the Gospel of St. John: "If someone loves me, he will keep my word, and my Father will love him, and we will come to him, and make our dwelling in him" (Jn. 14:23). The indwelling of the Father, the Son and the Spirit is the fundamental reality underlying all Christian life; and the summit of Christian perfection consists in living in perfect awareness of this profound intimacy with the life of the living God. The three divine Persons are reached through love, hope and faith. In the

151

love of the Spirit, the Father and the Word are known. In hope the Father anticipates our eternal encounter with him, so that in him we already meet the Word and the Paraclete. Faith makes us hear the Word from the Father and keep it under the guidance of the Holy Spirit. Thus the substance of chastity, poverty and obedience is the Spirit, the Father and the Son.

* * *

This opens a perspective that may help us to understand the meaning of these three virtues. If they are simply translations, in the order of behavior, of the theocentric Christian experience, and if this experience is essentially relative to the Father, the Son and the Spirit, it follows that these virtues are common and essential to all Christian life.

I will begin with the virtue of chastity, being well aware that it is especially questioned today, and that there are great misunderstandings of its traditional meaning in Catholic thought. At the same time, modern researches in the area of sexuality should throw some light upon it.

As it has often been understood, especially under the influence of St. Augustine's views on the nature of sinful concupiscence, chastity has meant, in a strict sense, control of sexual impulses, and, in a broader sense, restrictions of social contacts with "the other sex" in order to avoid anything that could remotely lead to unlawful relationships. Thus we have arrived at the following notion, borrowed from a spiritual book by a religious founder of the 19th century: "The greatest proof that I can give God of my love for him, is to renounce for him every affection, ever legitimate, through chastity." Similar ideas would be found in the writings of many founders and in many volumes studying the nature of the religious life. The result has been a negative instead of a positive approach to chastity, understood as a restriction rather than as a liberation; and when it was seen as liberating, this has been often implied as a downgrading of the sacrament of matrimony and the married life.

Yet this is contrary to our previous argument that chastity really means love. It is freedom, not restriction; relationship, not absence of relationship; affection, not stifling of affection; openness, not closing up of oneself.

Love is a matter of relationships. And chastity is the proper relationship of oneself to the world and especially to men. It cannot be opposed to marriage, unless marriage is seen in a Manichean light as something evil—a conception which influenced St. Augustine and has marked much of the popular theology of the religious life. This is a far cry from the point of view of traditional Catholic mysticism, which reads the *Canticle of Canticles* and its love poems as the story of the soul's relationship to God. St. Bernard and the Cistercians understood the monastery to be a school of love. St. John of the Cross wrote to a girl: "Love is the only goal for which you were created." And St. Thérèse of Lisieux wanted to push her identification with mankind in love to the point of "sitting at the table of sinners": "Lord, your child has understood your divine light; she begs forgiveness for her brothers; she agrees to be eating the bread of sorrow as long as you wish, and she does not want to rise from this table full of bitterness where the poor sinners are eating, until the day that you have decided upon: Have pity on us, Lord, for we poor sinners. Lord, send us away justified! . . ."[3]

3. *Manuscrits Autobiographiques,* Lisieux, 1957, p. 251.

Chastity is the practical application of love. Love regulates man's relationships to other men. It is according to his love that man meets and makes friend with others, that he gives himself, that he establishes a web of human ties, that he develops affections and friendships. The more we love, the more numerous will be those with whom we have a relationship of love, and the deeper will this relationship be. The sacramentality of marriage implies that the most profound relationship between human beings, that of man and woman in marriage, is a source of mutual sanctification, to the point that each partner becomes a sacramental channel of grace for the other, speaks the Word of God to the other, hears the Word from the other, embodies the guidance of the Spirit. The chastity of marriage manifests the exclusive character of this love-relationship. On the contrary, the chastity of consecrated celibacy is related, not to the exclusive depth of a unique relationship, but to the all-embracing scope of a universal relationship.

The scholastics divided love into two: love of friendship (*amor amicitiae*) and love of desire (*amor concupiscentiae*). Both belong to the same fundamental structure of the soul, which orients itself always toward that which it sees as good (*bonum*). Friendship orients toward men, so that I may give myself to them; desire orients toward things, so that I may acquire them, and be able to give them to those I love. Thus love is fundamentally one, although it can direct itself toward possession of that which should not be possessed, whether it be things or human beings. In any case, it includes sex as a means of communion and self-gift (in *amor amicitiae*) or as a means of possession and selfishness (in *amor concupiscentiae*).

The insight of contemporary depth psychology is the reverse of this. Sex, as understood by Freud and his disciples, is not simply one organ and one function, but the fundamental driving force (*libido*) behind all human actions. All human activity, all men's dreams, all men's ambitions, all men's achievements, are rooted in the power to communicate and relate oneself which is expressed in the mind as love and in the body as sex. All human relationships are, from this point of view, sexual, even when they take place at the highest level of spirituality. This is where the classical concept of chastity, in its narrowness, tallies with depth psychology: chastity, conceived as self-control especially in the area of sex, requires mutual fidelity among the married, and total abstinence among the unmarried; consecrates voluntary celibacy with a vow among the religious; and binds the clergy, at least in the Latin rite, with the obligation of celibacy. This concept is too narrow. Yet the error was not to relate chastity and sex, but to understand this tie too literally. Just as sex in the modern sense is universal and commands all our actions, orienting the psychology of a man differently from that of a woman, love (in the older or theological sense) is universal and opens a human being to the entire purpose of God over the whole universe. "My love is my weight," as Augustine said: it drags me down or pulls me up according to the level at which I love. Whether we call this *amor,* love, as theology would, or *libido,* with depth psychology, it corresponds to the fundamental desire of man to become "God by participation," and therefore to share God's universal presence by becoming one with him in the creatures he has made, and by pursuing his reflection in the attractions we feel to the human beings we love. The love which makes a person choose consecrated celibacy is the same as that which makes another choose marriage to a given person. Only the expression of that love differs.

In these conditions, I would find it inconceivable, in our century, to try and train young people for a life of consecrated celibacy without giving them the knowledge of the biological and psychological substratum of love which has been gained from depth psychology. If it is true—and I do not see how it could be denied—that conscious decisions have been influenced by unconscious ones, which have themselves their roots in our early relationships to the persons we have known and loved, or hated, then the decision for celibacy in the religious life derives from obscure motivations, the roots of which go back to one's early childhood. The important point is not where they ultimately originate in the depths of our personality, but that they may become free and voluntary, that the unconscious can become conscious, that what may have pushed us at the beginning be finally freely accepted and assumed as part of God's providential design upon us. Thus renunciation of sex will not be stinted, as it too often is, into renunciation of love; and will not be misrepresented as the choice of a higher love, when it should only be a different form of love.

When it is presented in this light, the virtue of chastity is a universal virtue, which enlarges the soul and makes it able to love to the utmost of its capacity. It expresses the universal desire for identity with all creation, in which the magical relationship to the world and to men for possession is overcome and replaced by self-giving to the created world of men and women, made as the images of God, and of things made as his shadows. Thomas Traherne wrote the following lines in its light:

Your enjoyment of the world is never right, till you so esteem it that everything in it is more your treasure than a King's exchequer full of gold and silver. And that exchequer yours also in its place and service. Can you take too much joy in your Father's works? He is himself in everything. Some things are little on the outside and rough and common, but I remember the time when the dust of the streets were as precious as gold to my infant eyes, and now they are more precious to the eye of reason.[4]

The religious has vowed chastity. This means that he has vowed love. He has vowed to love all men, not in their abstraction as mankind, but in the concrete personalities of the men whom he would meet. He has vowed to enter into a spiritual relationship with every man and every woman. In so doing, he is led by the Spirit, who is the Spirit of love.

* * *

The virtue of poverty is essentially related to God the Father, in that it is the practical sequel of theological hope. Hope implies that we look forward to the eschatological consummation of all things, when finally God will be all in all, when the transparence of the created world to his presence will be unimpaired, when no screen will separate man from the One from whom he comes and to whom he goes, when the beginning will coincide with the end. It is significant that St. Paul, describing this hope and its consummation, joins the experience of prayer to it: "I consider that the sufferings of the present time cannot be compared with the glory that is to be revealed in us. For creation expects with eager longing the revelation of the children of God: if it was

4. *Centuries,* I, 25, London, 1963, p. 13. See Paul Evdokimov: *Les Ages de la Vie Spirituelle,* Paris, 1964.

made subject to vanity—not by its own fault, but because of the one who subjected it—it is with the hope of being also freed from the slavery of corruption to enter the freedom of the glory of the children of God" (Rom. 8:20–21). This is hope seen on the cosmic scale: the expectation of the Day of the Lord by all creation, now subject to sin and corruption, but destined to share the liberty of the glory of the children of God. Paul adds, a few verses below:

Likewise the Spirit comes to the help of our weakness; for we do not know how to pray as we ought to; but the Spirit himself intercedes for us with unutterable groanings, and the One who scans the hearts knows the Spirit's desire, and that his intercession for the saints corresponds to God's design. [Rom. 8:26–27]

In this perspective, the virtue of poverty has little to do with wealth. Those who, toward the end of the Old Testament, were called the "poor" of the Lord, may or may not have been wealthy; the main point was that they made themselves poor before God:

> From the depths I cry to you, Yahweh;
> Lord, hear my cry!
> Make your ear attentive
> to the cry of my prayer!
>
> If you retain faults, Yahweh,
> Lord, who will subsist?
> But with you there is forgiveness;
> then there is fear of you.
>
> I hope in Yahweh, my soul hopes;
> I rely on his word,
> my soul relies on the Lord
> more than a watchman on the dawn!

May the watchman rely on the dawn,
and Israel on Yahweh!
For with Yahweh there is graciousness;
with him there is overflowing redemption;
he will ransom Israel
from all its faults. [Ps. 130]

Poverty should be understood in this light today. It means relying on the Father, turning to him, having him always in sight, seeking him ever; in a word it means praying. Only in prayer can we present ourselves before God destitute. When the Gospel according to Matthew says: "Blessed are the poor in spirit, for theirs is the Kingdom of heaven" (5:3), it implies that the poor in spirit have no kingdom of their own. They have rejected the Devil of the third temptation, who offered them the kingdoms of this world. They have preferred to have no kingdom, to be in the hands of the living God, to have their citizenship in heaven.

The history of the Church has seen a number of heresies deny the Church the right to ownership. Thus the Spiritual Franciscans identified the expectation of the Kingdom of God with the total abandonment of every earthly possession. Traditionally, in medieval monasteries, poverty did not mean the absence of goods, but their collective or corporate sharing and their being placed at the disposal of the wider Christian community. In the same way, the Fathers of the Church taught that ownership of the goods of this world meant, in the Christian context, stewardship, so that wealth, whether we have much or little of it, is employed for the Kingdom of God and shared with those who do not possess any or who possess less. But stewardship is only the consequence of a filial relationship to God which is manifested first of all in prayer and contemplation.

159

In prayer we take our littleness and place it at the disposal of the Father to do what he likes with it; we renounce what we think we are in order to become what we truly are; we abandon our human self-appreciation to rely on the appreciation of God, which we cannot know; we renounce having in order to be; we give up being oneself in order to reach the state of being-with-God; our presonality finds stability in not-being, in becoming, in the movement which St. Gregory of Nyssa called *epectasis,* the pilgrimage of man toward the perfection of the unknowable God; our personality finds stability in not-being, in becoming, in Pelagian or Semi-Pelagian, for a Pelagian prayer implies a contradition and is therefore not a prayer at all. There, only, is man really man, for man is to be defined by his interrelationships. He is most fully related to the Father, from whom he comes and to whom he goes, in the experience of the prophet Elijah: Yahweh is not in the hurricane, in the earthquake, in the fire; he is in the whisper of a light wind. The Father does not show himself in the hurricane of ambition, in the earthquake of acquisitiveness, in the fire of selfishness: he comes in silence.

The fulfillment of poverty is reached in the dialectic of posession and dispossession which has been described by the mystics:

> *I opened to my beloved,*
> *but my beloved had turned and gone.*
> *My soul failed me when he spoke.*
> *I sought him but found him not;*
> *I called him but he gave no answer.* [Cnt. 5:6]

Or, in a poem by Gregory of Narek:

> *Because I take shelter in this luminous confidence,*
> *vanquished I stand;*

160

knocked down, I win;
lost, I follow the path of the life-giving return.[5]

St. John of the Cross's poem, *The Dark Night,* describes this dialectic of the nothing and the all, in which man finds all by having and being nothing. The liturgy of the Easter Vigil exploits this theme of the "night which is my light in my delights" (*nox illuminatio mea in deliciis meis;* see Ps. 139:11).

Religious poverty, or, simply, Christian poverty, is the self-emptiness carved into the Christian soul by life led according to the virtue of hope, by relying on the Father alone. In other words, one is prepared for it, not by learning the rules and regulations of any religious community about the use of money (the early Franciscans were forbidden to touch money!), or finding out from moralists when the use of money without permission becomes a venial sin or turns into a mortal sin. Such a legalism should have nothing to do with the virtue of poverty. We prepare ourselves for poverty when we learn to pray. "He was praying in a certain place; and when he ceased, one of his disciples said to him: Lord, teach us to pray, as John taught his disciples. And he said to them: When you pray, say: Father, hallowed be your name. Your kingdom come. Give us each day our daily bread; and forgive us our sins, for we ourselves forgive everyone who is indebted to us; and lead us not into temptation" (Lk. 11:1–4).

Such an initiation into prayer should have two facets: it should be liturgical and contemplative.

Since the prayer of religious is that of a community—whether it is said in common or not makes no difference here—it should be essentially liturgical, patterned on and espousing the forms of

5. *Le Livre de Prières,* p. 101.

161

the Church's liturgy. There should be as few as possible of these devotional prayers added to the central liturgy of the Eucharist which have been multiplied in some communities. The purpose of liturgical prayer is to open ourselves so that we may participate totally in the Church's abundant life. It makes no sense that we should need to identify ourselves with another community of prayer than that of the Church, and that we should perpetuate the fiction that communities exist somehow as distinct and separate from the People of God.

Liturgical prayer should occasion an opening of ourselves to God in contemplation, this word being taken in a broad sense. The formation of the religious to prayer should therefore stress contemplative rather than petitionary prayer. To be poor means to expect nothing, therefore to ask for nothing. The proper attitude before God is not one of begging, but of adhesion to the mysteries of his will. This is an object for contemplation rather than petition. What counts is that which we may gain insight into, not that which we imagine we ought to receive. We should therefore prepare ourselves to encounter God in our living experience of his life, which is shared with us through the sacraments, into which we are introduced through the liturgy, and where our life will reach its acme. The summit of all life is the interchange that takes place in the eternity of the Father, the Son and the Spirit. This should be the model and goal of our prayer, the fulfillment of our poverty. An anonymous spiritual book written in the Rhineland in the 14th century begins with these words: "Spiritual poverty is a God-likeness. What is God? God is a being detached from all creatures. He is a free power, a pure act. In the same way spiritual poverty is a state of being detached from all creatures. And what is detachment? That which clings to nothing. Spiritual poverty clings to nothing and nothing to it."[6] Starting from the nothingness of poverty, the *nada* of John of the Cross, it ends with the corresponding *todo* which fills the void created by poverty in the soul: "Finally the soul attains to an everlasting entrance into the Godhead. Here God leads her with himself, makes her one love with himself, and thus man becomes one love with God . . ."

This is the ultimate object of the virtue of poverty: to be poor so that God may make us rich.

* * *

We now come to the last of the three religious virtues, obedience, which we have already connected with faith and with the Word of God. Obedience is the virtue of faith in practice, for it is nothing else than an awareness of the Word of God speaking to us through human media. If indeed God, through the Holy Spirit, may communicate with us directly in the depths of our being, he also uses human society and the circumstances of our life to make his will known to us, to attract us, to direct and orient our thoughts and our actions. In the context of the Catholic hierarchical concept of the Church, obedience takes on a universal meaning and has universal application. For the entire People of God willingly recognizes the authority of the hierarchy; and the hierarchy in turn, in the collegial understanding of its function, recognizes the charismatic authority wielded by the People and occasionally manifested through the prophetic personalities of the saints.

6. C. F. Kelley (ed.): *The Book of the Poor in Spirit,* New York, 1954, p. 53.

Once again, obedience is a Catholic quality, an attribute of the Catholic mind, a perfection assiduously pursued by those who want to "feel with the Church." It is not reserved to religious and to the relationship of authority within religious communities.

The theology of obedience, and especially of religious obedience, however, can be understood in different ways. The most common interpretation of it is no doubt that which Pope Paul VI used in his address to religious of May 23, 1966:

> Religious obedience is and must remain a holocaust of one's own will which is offered to God. A religious makes this sacrifice of self with a view to humbly obeying lawful superiors (whose authority, of course, should always be exercised within the confines of charity and with due regard for the human person), even though our times summon religious to the performance of many and heavy burdens, and to carrying out these duties more cheerfully and more promptly.

This sacrificial notion of obedience is also embodied in the Council's decree: "In professing obedience, religious offer the full surrender of their own will as a sacrifice of themselves to God, and so are permanently and securely united to God's salvific will" (art. 14).

I have quoted these important texts in order to emphasize the strength and value of this view of obedience, although I will now present another understanding of it. It is significant that Pope Paul joins to obedience a reference to authority and its exercise. For obedience and authority are correlative realities. The nature and qualities of obedience depend on the nature and qualities of authority. In the Pope's words, authority should take account of the demands of "charity" and of the "human person," that is, of justice. An exercise of authority which would pay no attention to these would be an abuse, and therefore would be in itself morally unjustified and undeserving of obedience. For obedience must be a human act, that is, a reasonable act. The concept of "blind obedience" or, in the paradoxical words of St. Ignatius Loyola, the practice of obeying "like a corpse," are self-contradictory. An obedience which is blind to the issues raised by the order given is irresponsible; and a corpse does not obey. Obedience therefore cannot mean doing something without incurring the responsibility of its consequences, this responsibility being attached only to the one who gave the order and not to the executors of the proposed action. It does not free the obedient person from moral responsibility for what he does. The consequence of this is that there cannot be a proper act of obedience without a judgment on the order given. Only a reasonable order may be carried out. In other words, the obligation of obedience is relative to the reasonable character of authority.

Furthermore, in a collegial conception of the Church, authority is not a one-way passage. Not only does the hierarchy wield functional authority over the People of God; the People of God in turn wields charismatic authority over the hierarchy. The exercise of authority must itself be an act of obedience to the promptings of the Spirit, which may be manifested through the smallest of the brethren. For authority is destined to serve the good of the whole body, not to inflate the ego of those who are sitting in its chairs. The reasonableness of its use depends on the superiors' readiness to read the signs of the times, to perceive the hints given by the Spirit, and on their insight into the spiritual universe of those over whom they preside, for their orders, given from the outside, should not contradict the guidance given to their subjects by the interior Spirit.

In this correlation of reasonable authority and reasonable obedience, there may well come to the surface many knots difficult to untie, and many minor or even major conflicts between what seem to be the demands of authority and what may also be the exigencies of the freedom of the children of God. This is where the unity of authority and obedience is manifested as being in the first place a unity in faith. Both authority and obedience must be acts of faith, though not because their object would somehow become object of faith. They are not acts of faith from the point of view of whatever exterior action has been ordered, but from that of their interior purpose and of the spiritual vision in which they are inserted. In ultimate analysis, only the Word of God deserves to be obeyed. He may speak through the hier-archic authority of the Church or of a religious community; he may also speak through the charisms of the faithful in the Church and in the communities. Response to him is obedience; and readiness to respond requires what has been called in Catholic spirituality "discernment of spirits." To obey is to believe that the Word has been heard. Yet neither superior nor subject may be certain beforehand that the Word will speak each time authority is exercised. No one knows, before an order is given, if that order deserves to be obeyed. Only when the reception of an order coincides with the ecstatic recognition that the Word speaks should obedience follow. This puts an all but intolerable burden on authority: it is an awesome responsibility to have to speak the Word, for who knows if the Word will use our words to manifest himself? Yet this is also where authority in the Church, and likewise in a religious community, becomes light: if we are not sure that the Word will use our authority, then we should not try to speak with authority; we should not give orders; we should only offer advice and suggestions; we should

listen so that we may speak. Thus authority and obedience dove-
tail to the point where they constitute only one reality: the reality
of collegial action, the community of minds, the organic consensus
of the many who together constitute one cell in the Body of Christ.

Training for obedience should therefore be also a training for
authority. It should be focussed essentially on faith and its profound desire to hear and to follow the Word. Far from it to be
an exercise in blindness, for it should prepare for insight. It
should never stoop to giving senseless orders and to make human persons perform childish actions. It should on the contrary
treat subjects (even novices) as human beings who deserve respect and therefore should not be humiliated through the performance of meaningless and unreasonable actions. From the
point of view of "the sacrifice of the will," obedience to such
orders may be justified; but the giving of such orders may
never be condoned, for it contradicts the order of justice. The
rules and customs of religious communities must respect the
higher rules of the natural dignity of the human person and of
the supernatural freedom of the children of God. The Epistle to
the Hebrews notes that Christ, "Son though he was, learnt obedience through his sufferings" (5:8). That is to say, obedience
comes from experience. There is no substitute for experience in
learning obedience, for experience provides insight into the trans-
parency of the human words we hear, so that the Word may
shine through them. The possibility of obedience is also the possibility of liberation. "May you hear his voice today" (Ps. 95:7).

*　*　*

I have tried to show the three virtues which are often, in religious communities, consecrated by three vows, in their univer-

sal revelance to Christian life rather than in their narrow application to religious life. For I am convinced that religious orders today should cultivate their links with the People of God as a whole rather than their singular characteristics. The signs of the times call for a return to the classical sources of spiritual life in order to become more and more members of the People rather than a class set apart. This can be done only by developing the elements of common life that will tie religious communities with the total experience of the Church. Reflection on the vows and the corresponding virtues should hold a prominent place in this process of universalization, by which our life-beat will follow the Catholic heart of the whole Church.

The three virtues of chastity, poverty and obedience mean love, hope and faith, which relate us to, and give us a share of, the life of the Spirit, the Father and the Word: the Spirit who attracts man and urges him interiorly toward fellowship with other men; the Father whose overflowing being fills those who come to him empty; the Word who uses human words and human experiences to speak to men.

VII.

The Mystery of the Church in the Liturgical Constitution

THE CLOSE interrelationships of the various constitutions and decrees of the IInd Vatican Council will make it necessary to study these documents together rather than separately. On the one hand, each is couched in a certain language patterned according to a certain structure, which provide their own meaning. On the other hand, each document of the Council is destined to constitute one factor in a total renovation of the Church. From this common purpose they all derive a common spirit. As a result, it will be necessary to study the ecumenical mind of the Council not only in the Decree on Ecumenism, but also in the broad Catholic orientation of the Liturgical Constitution, in the ecclesiology of the *De Ecclesia* and in the relevance of the *De Revelatione* to one of the major ecumenical problems of today. In the same way, the ecclesiology of the Council will be found, not only in the Constitution on the Church—although it is mainly there—but also in the Decree on Ecumenism, in the

Constitution on the Liturgy, and in what the *De Revelatione* says and implies about the presence of Christ in the Scriptures wherever these are read with faith and with the desire to follow the mind of the Church and the interior testimony of the Spirit.

The Constitution on the Liturgy presents a rather full approach to the mystery of the Church, which is no other than the paschal mystery commemorated and re-enacted in the Eucharistic action. As is normal in a document destined to prepare the reform of the liturgy, the topic of the Church is not treated for itself; yet it is evidently impossible to speak of the theology of worship without referring to a theology of the Church. In fact, all this document assumes a certain view of the Church, which I will try to outline here.

* * *

"From the side of Christ in the dormition of the cross there came forth the admirable sacrament of the whole Church" (art. 5). The birth of the Church is viewed as the first-fruit of the death of Christ on the cross; and this death is presented in the language of a dormition, analogous to the dormition of Adam, out of whose side Eve was formed. In the context of this passage, the appearance of the Church under the symbol of the poured blood and water from the side of Christ is an anticipation of the resurrection. Thus the Church is radically related to the death and resurrection of Christ; she is the counterpart of Eve, "mother of all the living"; her function is soteriological, for it is from the humanity of Christ, as "the instrument of our salvation" (art. 5), that she proceeds at the very moment when salvation is being acquired in the mystery of the dormition of Christ.

In keeping with this starting point, the Liturgical Constitution sees the Church always in the perspective of the paschal mystery. As article 6 points out, "the Church has never failed to come together to celebrate the paschal mystery." This is not only because, as is mentioned at the beginning of this number, the apostles were sent "to accomplish the work of salvation, which they proclaimed, by means of the sacrifice and of the sacraments"; it is also because those who enter the Church through baptism are thereby initiated to "the paschal mystery of Christ." The "whole Church" born on Calvary was therefore not simply the Church as the structure of salvation; it was also the Church in its single members: all were born through the water and the blood, that is, through Baptism and the Holy Eucharist flowing from the side of Christ.

This relationship between the Church, each Christian and the mystery of Easter is exemplified in the "memorial" character of our participation in the Last Supper. "At the Last Supper, on the night when he was betrayed, our Saviour instituted the Eucharistic sacrifice of his body and blood, in which the sacrifice of the cross would be perpetuated through the centuries in view of his coming again, and in which the memorial of his death and resurrection would be entrusted to the Church, his beloved bride" (art. 47). The Last Supper, in its sacramental memorial as in its original setting, is the wedding feast in the course of which the Church receives the pledge that makes her the bride of Christ. This pledge is the Eucharist, "sacrament of piety, token of unity, bond of love, paschal banquet in which Christ is eaten, the mind is filled with grace and a promise of future glory is given us" (art. 47). The Eucharist is the permanent epiphany of Christ, in which the marriage of the Lamb is performed and the Spirit and the Bride say "come." Or, in the words of the constitution, "in this great work in which God is given perfect glory and men are sanctified, Christ always unites to himself the Church, his most beloved bride, who invokes her Lord and, through him, offers worship to the Eternal Father" (art. 7).

The first image of the Church and the first title by which she is known is that of bride. This is in the line of the prophetic concept of Israel as the bride of God in the Old Testament; it also follows the theology of St. Paul in his Epistle to the Ephesians (5:25 ff.) and the Apocalypse. One may also note the correspondence between this emphasis on the Church as the bride and the description of the Church, in Chapter I of the constitution *De Ecclesia,* as "the spotless bride of the spotless Lamb" (art. 6). In biblical imagery, the image of the bride is germane to that of the banquet-feast and also to the image of the "house" that will be built through the bride's fecundity. The parallelism of the Church, "mother of the faithful," and of Eve, "mother of the living," belongs to the same order of thought.

The Church is also the Body of Christ. The constitution associates this scriptural representation of the Church with the exercise of the priesthood of Christ: "Rightly the liturgy is held to be the performance of the priestly office of Jesus Christ, in which the sanctification of man is signified by perceptible signs and the whole public worship is performed by the mystical body of Jesus Christ, in its Head and members" (art. 7). In the next sentence, the liturgical celebration is described as "the work of Christ the priest and of his body which is the Church." The "body which is the Church," as St. Paul calls it, is "mystical" in so far as it includes the "Head and members," who, according to the traditional meaning of "Mystical Body," have been made one in the "mystery" of the Eucharist. All the sacraments also are

172

"destined to the upbuilding of the Body of Christ" (art. 59), thus increasing its mystical or mystery-elaborated nature.

The Church, which is the Bride of Christ and his Body, has a specific function to fulfill in relation to the salvation of mankind. In the soteriological perspective of the "mystery," which is that of the Constitution on the Liturgy, the task of the Church is essentially relative to salvation. We therefore are invited to view the Church's action from a spiritual, dynamic or pneumatological angle rather than merely from the standpoint of its institutional structure and the specific responsibilities of the magisterium. The Church's task, "before men can come to the liturgy" (art. 9), is that of "announcing to non-believers the good tidings of salvation." It includes the kerygma concerning "the only true God and the one whom he sent, Jesus Christ"; it also includes a call to penance and conversion. But the Church's mission of preaching the Gospel does not end once men have received Baptism. Faith and penance must be constantly preached to the faithful themselves, who must be invited to receive the sacraments, taught all that Christ commanded, called to the works of love, of piety, of apostolate.

This pre-liturgical task of the Church climaxes in the liturgy, "the summit to which the Church's action is directed and the source from which all its value flows" (art. 10). All Christian activity reaches its peak when "all, being children of God by faith and Baptism, gather into one, praise God in the midst of the assembly, partake of the sacrifice and eat the Lord's Supper" (art. 10). The Church is this assembly where the children of God are gathered into one; she is the *cahal* of the Hebrews in the wilderness, the People leaving Egypt for the land promised to Abraham their Father, the Remnant eating the sacred meal together and recognizing the Lord at the breaking of bread. This is, equivalently, the realm of salvation, which all Christian activity must extend, and the spiritual house that it must build up. The liturgy, in which the Covenant is passed and the death and resurrection of Christ is mystically present, is therefore the source of all Christian virtue, which draws the faithful to show in themselves the eager love felt by Christ for mankind (art. 10).

It follows that the Church, which is already the bride, the Body, the assembly, becomes Christ's instrument for the praise of God the Father. This praise does not come only from the faithful. The Lord also interprets the laudatory intention of all visible creation, bringing its expression up to heaven; and, by a reverse movement, he brings down on earth the eternal hymn sung to the glory of the Father by the invisible creation. This doxological function of Christ, as described in article 83, is fulfilled "through his Church itself," which "praises the Lord unceasingly and intercedes for the salvation of the whole world" (art. 83). In this spiritual concert of creation, relayed by the Church, we may hear "the voice of the bride speaking to the Bridegroom and even the prayer of Christ, with his Body, to the Father" (art. 84). All those who, in the Church, associate themselves to this praise, in turn share in the highest honor of the bride and "stand before the throne of God in the name of Mother Church" (art. 85).

This liturgical function of praise, by which the Church on earth is associated to heaven, brings us to the double aspect of the Church. She is on earth, locally materialized in parishes or local communities which "somehow represent the visible Church spread throughout the world" (art. 42). In her there is "a variety of nations and peoples" (art. 37) and "legitimate varieties and adaptations to different groups, regions and peoples" (art. 38). This earthly, spread out, visible aspect of the Church in her pilgrim state on earth corresponds to a heavenly aspect. The visible liturgy implies a "participation in and a foretaste of the heavenly liturgy celebrated in the heavenly Jerusalem to which we journey as pilgrims, where Christ is sitting at the right hand of God, a minister of the Holies and of the true Tabernacle" (art. 8). The Church is thus also the heavenly Jerusalem, singing the hymn of glory with the heavenly hosts.

The two aspects of the Church are carefully described. It belongs to "the genuine nature of the true Church" to be "both human and divine, visible and yet with invisible qualities, eager in action yet devoted to contemplation, present in the world and yet on pilgrimage, so that the human is directed and subordinated to the divine, the visible to the invisible, action to contemplation, the present to the future city that we seek" (art. 2). The unity of the human and the divine implies a tension from the human toward the divine in the Church, which defines her eschatological orientation toward the total fulfillment of what is only partially given in her. This tension makes the Church the eschatological sign "raised above the nations" (art. 2), calling "the dispersed children of God to unity until there be one fold and one shepherd" (art 2). In the Bible and in early Christian literature, the Shepherd leads his flock through the final exodus from this world, bringing all things back to the Father.

Clearly, this is the ultimate dimension of the paschal mystery, in which the liturgy introduces us ever anew, re-creating the Church everyday.

* * *

The Constitution on the Liturgy, this should be evident, cannot replace the Constitution on the Church, which develops each

point thoroughly in its description of the collegial and the eschatological status of the Church, the two foci around which it is
organized. But it will take time for the implications of the *De
Ecclesia* to be perceived. Some of them may be set in a more
vivid light by the intimate connection of the mystery of the
liturgical presence of the Lord and that of his relationship to the
Church which is his bride and his Body. Thus the liturgical
reform should attune the faithful to the aspects of the mystery of
the Church which are best exemplified in liturgical participation. Meditation on the Constitution on the Liturgy will help
to understand the *De Ecclesia* in depth. It will help us to read it
as a scriptural and patristic document destined to lead us into
the mystery of Emmanuel rather than as a canonical pronouncement.